NATO

THE DANGEROUS DINOSAUR

TED GALEN CARPENTER

Paperback ISBN: 978-1-948647-61-8
Hardback ISBN: 978-1-948647-62-5
eBook ISBN: 978-1-948647-63-2

Library of Congress Cataloging-in-Publication Data available.

Printed in the United States of America.

Cover design: Jon Meyers

Cato Institute
1000 Massachusetts Ave., NW
Washington, DC 20001
www.cato.org

To my grandchildren: Carson, Savannah, Julian, Miranda, and Ella. May you all survive NATO's unnecessary and dangerous ambitions.

CONTENTS

ACKNOWLEDGMENTS

I owe a considerable debt of gratitude to so many people who made this book possible. As usual, I'm grateful to the members of Cato's board of directors and to Cato's management team for consistently supporting my work over the past 34 years. They have always encouraged the Institute's defense and foreign policy scholars to identify what is wrong with America's foreign policy and play the role of constructive critics who offer worthy alternatives. *NATO: The Dangerous Dinosaur* is my latest contribution to that ongoing, very important effort. Thanks are also owed to Jason Kuznicki, Eleanor O'Connor, Jon Meyers, and the other members of Cato's editorial and book production staff for handling the logistics to produce another fine product.

Special appreciation goes out to Christopher A. Preble, vice president for defense and foreign policy studies, and John Glaser, director of foreign policy studies, for guiding this book project and offering numerous constructive suggestions along the way. I'm also grateful to several other scholars, including Doug Bandow, Ivan Eland, Christopher Layne, and Walter A. McDougall, for their helpful comments. A sizable scholarly community has developed over the past few decades to support a new, much more prudent U.S. foreign policy based on realism and restraint. In addition to the individuals mentioned above, such impressive analysts as John Mearsheimer, Andrew Bacevich, Jack F. Matlock, Stephen M. Walt,

Barry R. Posen, Richard K. Betts, Robert W. Merry, and many others have provided trenchant critiques of NATO's misguided policies since the end of the Cold War.

That intellectual milieu has aided me greatly in preparing the books, journal articles, and opinion pieces I've written through the years about NATO. But I also owe a great debt to two other individuals who guided me during the early stages of my career. Professor Robert A. Divine, a renowned historian of 20th century U.S. foreign policy, supervised my PhD dissertation and broadened my perspective regarding that field's many complexities. The late Professor David F. Healy supervised my thesis for my master of arts degree and was my first true mentor. His professional guidance, as well as the rigorous scholarship he exhibited in two excellent books of his own on U.S. imperialism, greatly influenced my thinking. Both dedicated scholars emphasized the importance of questioning the conventional wisdom on important issues and daring to present unorthodox, or even unpopular, interpretations if the evidence warranted such conclusions. I have never forgotten those lessons.

Most of all, I appreciate more than words can express the loving support that my wife, Barbara, has given me throughout this and so many other book projects. Her insightful suggestions are exceeded only by her patience. Finally, I am honored to receive the affection and admiration of my grandchildren, Carson, Savannah, Julian, Miranda, and Ella. This book is dedicated to them with the hope of a more peaceful future.

INTRODUCTION

BEYOND BURDEN SHARING

Donald Trump has emerged as the single biggest catalyst for a growing debate on both sides of the Atlantic about the future of the North Atlantic Treaty Organization (NATO) and U.S. policy regarding the alliance. His importance was apparent even before he became president. In his most definitive foreign policy speech during the 2016 presidential campaign, Trump asserted, "Our allies are not paying their fair share" of the collective defense effort. He added, "The countries we are defending must pay for the cost of this defense, *and if not, the U.S. must be prepared to let these countries defend themselves*."[1] Although the demand was couched in the context of traditional burden-sharing complaints, his comment suggested that the security commitment itself was not open ended or sacrosanct.

In July 2016, Trump indicated that whether the United States would defend the Baltic republics depended on whether they had fulfilled their alliance obligations. Asked during an interview with the *New York Times* if such NATO countries as Lithuania, Latvia, and Estonia could count on the United States to come to their aid in case of a Russian attack, Trump answered with a question: "Have they fulfilled their obligations to us?" He then stated that "if they fulfill their obligations to us, the answer is yes." Implicitly, if they had not done so, his answer would be "no." Indeed, Trump noted later, "We're talking about countries that are doing very well. Yes, I would be absolutely prepared to tell those countries,

'Congratulations, you will be defending yourself [sic].'" Reporters observed that Trump's comments sent "a chill through Europe."[2]

Both domestic and foreign supporters of the status quo—that is, those favoring a tight link between the security policies of the United States and Europe—reacted with both anger and apprehension. Sen. Lindsey Graham (R-SC) argued, "Statements like these make the world more dangerous and the United States less safe. I can only imagine how our allies in NATO, particularly the Baltic states, must feel after reading these comments from Mr. Trump. I'm 100 percent certain how Russian president Putin feels—he's a very happy man. The Republican nominee for President is essentially telling the Russians and other bad actors that the United States is not fully committed to supporting the NATO alliance."[3] NATO Secretary General Jens Stoltenberg implicitly rebuked Trump, emphasizing that, "Solidarity among Allies is a key value for NATO. This is good for European security and good for US security."[4]

Since he became president, Trump has diluted some of his more critical comments about NATO, and his administration's actual policies have not differed all that much from those of his predecessors. Indeed, some of his first actions as president were to walk back his earlier depiction of NATO as "obsolete" and to emphasize that he believed the alliance still served a crucial function. Members of Trump's foreign policy team went to even greater lengths to reassure the European allies.

Nevertheless, Trump's apparent ambivalence toward NATO, including the Article 5 commitment proclaiming that an attack on one member is an attack on all, has surfaced periodically since he entered the Oval Office. In January 2019, the *New York Times* broke a major story noting that, in conversations with other officials in 2018, Trump had indicated on several occasions a willingness to withdraw the United States from the alliance.[5] Again, though, it was unclear whether his comments constituted idle musings or serious consideration of an alternative grand strategy. Just days after the *New York Times* article appeared, Trump gave renewed assurances about his commitment to NATO, but once again did so in terms that emphasized his demand for greater burden sharing: "We will be with NATO 100 percent, but as I told the countries, you have to step up," he stated.[6]

Speculation about Trump's allegedly frosty attitude toward NATO beyond the burden-sharing issue exceeds the available evidence, however. On the eve of the May 2017 NATO summit, Brookings Institution scholar Thomas Wright observed, "President Trump is the only American president since NATO's founding who has not explicitly endorsed Article 5."[7] The president's coy stance at the summit itself did little to dispel the anxiety of staunch alliance supporters. Trump spoke of "the commitments that bind us together as one," but as his legion of critics on both sides of the Atlantic pointed out, he did not explicitly reaffirm Article 5.[8] An article in *Foreign Policy* asserted that Trump's comments about that commitment at a closed-door dinner following the main, public session left alliance leaders "appalled."[9]

The president's behavior before and during the July 2018 summit raised new questions about his respect for the NATO allies and the sincerity of his commitment to Article 5.[10] But alliance defenders habitually overstated the scope and nature of his criticisms. Once again, the source of his discontent was a perceived lack of burden sharing by the other NATO members. His goal was more serious, substantive defense efforts on the part of Washington's European security partners. Once they satisfied his wishes on that issue (at least rhetorically), Trump expressed fulsome praise for the alliance.

U.S. discontent with burden sharing is nothing new; indeed, it dates almost from NATO's birth. However, Washington's frustration appears to have grown in the years since the September 11, 2001, terrorist attacks. U.S. military spending nearly doubled during the following decade, whereas the already modest outlays of NATO's European members continued the downward trajectory that began with the end of the Cold War. Even before the emergence of Donald Trump, the issue was clearly becoming a growing source of annoyance to the United States.

Washington's Inconsistent Burden-Sharing Message

Unfortunately, there has been a persistent gap between the expressed desires of U.S. leaders for the European allies to take greater responsibility for collective defense efforts and tangible U.S. actions that encouraged the Europeans to do so. Indeed, as discussed in Chapter 5, U.S. officials have repeatedly pursued policies that discouraged and even undermined independent European security initiatives. Washington's actual behavior instead has fostered prolonged, excessive European dependence on America's security leadership and military exertions, even as U.S. burden-sharing complaints have continued to mount.

In NSC 82, Washington's primary defense guidance document regarding Europe during the early Cold War period, the Truman administration insisted that the European members of NATO would have to provide the bulk of the alliance's military personnel.[11] Yet the administration's 1951 decision to expand the U.S. occupation army in West Germany and station more than 100,000 additional troops on the Continent as part of a NATO defense force sent the opposite message. Granted, NATO's first supreme commander, Gen. Dwight D. Eisenhower, insisted the deployment was merely temporary, until the European nations had recovered enough to build sufficient forces of their own. He believed that such a result definitely should take place within 10 years.[12]

Contrary to Eisenhower's expectations, no withdrawal took place; instead, the size of the U.S. force gradually increased to more than 300,000. Indeed, even the post–Cold War downsizing of the U.S. military presence on the Continent was relatively modest. Washington's "temporary" step in 1951 created a sizable, long-term tripwire in the event of a Soviet offensive. Guaranteeing that American military personnel would be among the initial casualties in any war encouraged European complacency and a perpetual overreliance on U.S. protection—however uneasy the allies might be from time to time about their dependence.

Washington's verbal impatience at Europe's reluctance to bear a greater share of the collective defense responsibility has flared periodically. In late 1953, Secretary of State John Foster Dulles warned that the United States might have to conduct an "agonizing reappraisal" of its European security commitment if the allies didn't make a more serious effort.[13] From the beginning, though, U.S. officials sent contradictory messages to the allies about how seriously Washington regarded the importance of burden sharing. The massive troop deployment that accompanied Dulles's grousing was merely one example of that contradiction.

U.S. statements and actions have continuously undercut the official calls for the Europeans to boost their defense expenditures and undertake greater security responsibilities. Until the Trump administration, NATO's European members routinely dismissed such warnings, and they did so for a very basic reason. Alan Tonelson, former associate editor at *Foreign Policy*, aptly identified the inherent futility of Washington's burden-sharing approach. "U.S. leaders never gave the Europeans sufficient incentive to assume greater relative military responsibilities. The incentive was lacking, in turn, because Washington never believed it could afford to walk away from NATO or even reduce its role, if the allies stood firm. Worse, U.S. leaders repeatedly telegraphed that message to the Europeans—often in the midst of burden-sharing controversies."[14]

Despite his earlier rhetoric about seeking greater European self-reliance regarding defense, as president, Eisenhower actually increased the connection of America's security to that of the allies. His administration's doctrine of massive retaliation emphasized that the United States definitely would treat an attack on another NATO member the same as it would an attack on American territory. The U.S. response might even include an escalation to thermonuclear war. In the United States, the massive retaliation policy met with some criticism because of its dangerous inflexibility, but the NATO allies actually seemed relieved. The Eisenhower administration's stance reduced the danger that Washington would separate American and European security interests and objectives. Tight links, the Europeans assumed, also would make it less likely that the Soviet Union would seek to split the alliance and challenge the U.S. commitment.

President John F. Kennedy's administration in turn adopted a "flexible response" policy to replace the reliance on massive retaliation, and that worried NATO capitals. As Christopher Layne, the Robert M. Gates Chair in Intelligence and National Security at Texas A&M University, documents in his seminal book, *The Peace of Illusions: American Grand Strategy from 1940 to the Present*, NATO's European members sought multiple assurances of security solidarity.[15] U.S. officials obliged at nearly every opportunity. President Kennedy's secretary of defense, Robert S. McNamara, was categorical that there would be no waffling in Washington's commitment. "The United States is prepared to respond immediately with nuclear weapons to the use of nuclear weapons against one or more members of the alliance. The United States is also prepared to counter with nuclear weapons any Soviet conventional attack so strong that it cannot be dealt with by conventional means."[16]

Nevertheless, the allies seemed to remain nervous. As Layne notes, they feared that unless robust tripwire forces and weapons continued to be deployed, the United States and the Soviet Union (USSR) might strike an implicit deal in the event of war to confine the conflict to Moscow's East European satellite empire and NATO Europe, thereby putting the American and Soviet homelands off limits.[17] The allies' priorities, Layne contends, were the opposite. They hoped that if war broke out, the superpowers would primarily fight it over the heads of the European countries and spare their region most of the devastating consequences.

The only way to prevent Washington from delinking America's fortunes from those of its European allies in the event of a crisis was to insist on perpetuating a robust presence of U.S. ground forces. That measure demonstrated the inviolability of Washington's commitment, and it made a cynical U.S.-Soviet deal to spare the rival homelands nearly impossible. So, too, did the deployment of intermediate-range U.S. nuclear missiles during the 1980s—a move that allied governments embraced, despite the intense public opposition from pacifist factions in West European countries.

The presence of tripwire forces to ensure American casualties at the outset of any armed conflict in Europe is a key reason why the NATO allies still want U.S. military units on the Continent, long after the end of the Cold War. Such tripwires supposedly ensure that the United States will not (indeed cannot) renege on its security commitment to the allies. That certainty, in turn, supposedly maximizes the credibility of deterrence and makes a war in Europe improbable. The European desire for a renewed and enhanced U.S. tripwire has soared as worries mount about the intentions of Russian president Vladimir Putin's regime.

Despite prolific expressions of transatlantic security solidarity and the continued presence of U.S. tripwire forces, burden-sharing arguments have continued to plague NATO. As the January 5, 2019, *New York Times* obituary for Harold Brown, President Jimmy Carter's secretary of defense, recalled, "Concerned that America's allies were not sharing enough of the defense burden, Mr. Brown repeatedly urged the North Atlantic Treaty Organization . . . to increase military spending, but with limited success." In his final meeting with his NATO counterparts, "He had sharp valedictory words for the allies: 'They need to behave as if their military security is as important to them as it is to us.'"[18]

However, the U.S. message has remained as inconsistent and contradictory as ever. In June 2011, departing Secretary of Defense Robert M. Gates issued a candid admonition to the alliance partners. "The blunt reality is that there will be dwindling appetite and patience in the U.S. Congress, and in the American body politic writ large, to expend increasingly precious funds on behalf of nations that are apparently unwilling to devote the necessary resources . . . to be serious and capable partners in their own defense," he said in an address to a think tank in Brussels.[19]

At a meeting of NATO defense ministers in February 2014, Secretary of Defense Chuck Hagel warned his European counterparts that they must step up their commitment to the alliance or watch it become irrelevant. Declining European defense budgets, he emphasized, are "not sustainable. Our alliance can endure only as long as we are willing to fight for it, and invest in it." Rebalancing NATO's "burden-sharing and capabilities," Hagel stressed, "is mandatory—not elective." His tone was firm: "America's contributions in NATO remain starkly disproportionate, so adjustments in the U.S. defense budget cannot become an excuse for further cuts in European defense spending."[20]

Yet U.S. officials still go out of their way to reassure the European allies that Washington's commitment to NATO remains as steadfast as ever. That pattern has persisted during the Trump administration. The remarks that Vice President Mike Pence and Secretary of Defense James Mattis delivered at the annual Munich Security Conference in February 2017 signaled to European capitals that Trump's rhetoric about NATO being obsolete and the supposedly conditional nature of the U.S. security commitment should not be taken all that seriously. Pence stressed the permanence of the transatlantic security relationship:

> Today, on behalf of President Trump, I bring you this assurance. The United States of America strongly supports NATO and will be unwavering in our commitment to this transatlantic alliance. (Applause.) We've been faithful for generations—and as you keep faith with us, under President Trump we will always keep faith with you. Now, the fates of the United States and Europe are intertwined. Your struggles are our struggles. Your success is our success, and ultimately, we walk into the future together. This is President Trump's promise: We will stand with Europe, today and every day.[21]

Mattis insisted that for the United States, "Article 5 is a bedrock commitment." Moreover, Washington was taking new steps to underscore its commitment to the collective defense. "The United States is moving units into the Baltic states, Poland, Romania and Bulgaria, under Operation Atlantic Resolve." Lest anyone worry about the new administration's loyalty to NATO, Mattis added: "President Trump came into office and has thrown now his full support to NATO."[22]

One could scarcely imagine a set of statements from high-level U.S. officials less likely to induce greater burden sharing. The underlying message from the new administration was that, despite Trump's sometimes abrasive comments critical of NATO, very little of substance would change. The European allies could safely continue their longstanding free-riding ways. The problem for Pence, Mattis, and other passionate adherents to the status quo in transatlantic security policy is that both the roster of critics and the intensity of their criticisms are growing. The gap between the U.S. and European perspectives on burden sharing are becoming wider and more acrimonious.

U.S. officials point out that NATO members made a commitment at the 2006 summit (reiterated at the 2014 summit) to spend a minimum of 2 percent of their gross domestic product (GDP) on defense. At the time of the Ukraine crisis in 2014, other than the United States, only Britain and Greece (because of its worries about fellow NATO member Turkey) had met that goal. Since then, Estonia and Poland have done so—barely.

The other Eastern European nations, supposedly the most at risk of Russian intimidation or aggression, lag, sometimes far behind. As of July 2018, the other two Baltic republics, Lithuania and Latvia, are spending 1.7 and 1.8 percent, respectively. Romania devotes 1.8 percent; Bulgaria, 1.5 percent. Hungary and the Czech Republic bring up the rear at 1.1 percent. NATO's leading countries do no better. The figures for France and Italy are 1.8 and 1.1 percent, respectively. Perhaps most telling, democratic Europe's leading economic power, Germany, spends a mere 1.2 percent on defense.[23]

Burden-Sharing Disputes Are Not the Main Threat to the Alliance

The burden-sharing issue continues to capture the bulk of media attention, but criticisms of NATO among members of the American foreign policy community now go far beyond that familiar complaint. To some extent, such discontent reflects inevitable questions about the continued relevance to America's security of an alliance now entering its eighth decade and confronting a very different security environment than the one it was created to address. Moreover, the growing criticisms are not confined to this side of the Atlantic. European complaints about Washington's sometimes overbearing leadership style, its regional and global behavior, and U.S. policy priorities are on the rise.

The sources of discontent have grown as the United States has pushed NATO to become an offensive rather than a purely defensive security organization. The alliance now pursues military missions in arenas such as the Balkans, Afghanistan, the Middle East, and North Africa. All of those theaters lie outside—in some cases, far outside—NATO's original territorial concern. Such military missions also are vastly different from NATO's original purpose: defending Western Europe from possible aggression by the Soviet Union.

Most of the new intra-alliance tensions involve issues that are more substantive, pertinent, and intractable than the traditional burden-sharing squabbles. For example, the allies have frustrated Washington's determination, despite Russia's opposition and mounting anger, to continue expanding NATO eastward. France, Germany, and other key members adamantly oppose that step. Those recalcitrant NATO members appear to have drawn the line against offering membership to Georgia and Ukraine.

Indeed, disagreements within NATO about overall policy toward Moscow are substantial. The United States and most of the East European members favor a hard-line, confrontational policy, believing that such a stance is necessary to deter Russian aggression. But France, Hungary, Italy, Turkey, and other NATO powers advocate a more accommodating approach. They resist the notion of treating Russia as though it poses a security threat akin to what the USSR once posed. Turkey already has concluded a major arms deal with Moscow (over Washington's vehement objections). And there is proliferating discontent in NATO's ranks about continuing, much less intensifying, the system of economic sanctions that alliance members imposed on Russia following that country's annexation of Ukraine's Crimea Peninsula in 2014.

Beyond the issue of policy toward Russia, disagreements are growing between the United States and its European allies about how to deal with developments in the Middle East and other regions. The sharp split regarding Washington's undermining of the Joint Comprehensive Plan of Action—the multilateral agreement that placed restraints on Iran's nuclear program in exchange for loosening the array of economic sanctions against Tehran—is a graphic example. The European Union's leading powers have taken steps to preserve the fragile détente with Iran, even as the Trump administration continues to intensify its uncompromising posture toward that country's clerical regime.

Perhaps the most disruptive development, though, is the growth of authoritarian populism in several NATO countries. That process is the most advanced in Turkey, where the government of President Recep Tayyip Erdoğan has become a thinly disguised dictatorship. But similar trends are evident in Hungary and Poland, where governments seem to be inexorably eroding democratic institutions and values. The coalition government that swept into power during the 2018 elections in Italy exhibits some of the same behavior, and increasingly relevant populist parties in other NATO countries confirm that the trend may span the continent. If that process continues, U.S. leaders will be hard pressed to credibly portray NATO as an alliance of democratic powers. And how the American public will react if called upon to defend a treaty ally ruled by an ugly dictatorship is decidedly unclear.

That problem will grow worse if the alliance adds new members that have a weak commitment to democratic norms. Ukraine could be an especially troublesome case. Although Kiev's cheerleaders in Western (especially U.S.) media like to portray Ukraine as a beleaguered democratic David facing Russia's evil, dictatorial Goliath, the reality is far murkier and more unsettling, especially with respect to political values.

Yet supporters seem oblivious to Kiev's moral deficiencies. Moscow's portrayal of the 2014 Maidan Revolution as a U.S. coup that brought a fascist regime to power in Ukraine was simplistic and unfair. Ukraine's recently departed administration, led by Petro Poroshenko, did not fit such an extreme stereotype. Post-revolution elections appear to have been reasonably free and fair, and some major factions are committed to genuine democratic values. But Ukraine is hardly a model of Western-style democracy. Not only is it afflicted with extensive graft and corruption, but some extreme nationalist and even neo-Nazi groups play a significant role in the "new" Ukraine.[24] The notoriously fascist Azov Battalion, for example, continues to occupy a prominent position in Kiev's efforts to defeat separatists in Ukraine's eastern Donbass region. Other armed ultranationalist units are active on the eastern front, and some of those domestic militias seek to intimidate more moderate Ukrainians throughout the country.[25]

Even the Poroshenko government itself had adopted troubling censorship measures and other autocratic policies.[26] Officials in both Barack Obama's and Donald Trump's administrations have taken a much too casual attitude toward U.S. cooperation with a deeply flawed Ukrainian government. Worse, there is no indication that American policymakers have abandoned their goal of adding Ukraine to NATO. To the contrary, there are explicit signs that the bulk of the U.S. foreign policy establishment is more determined than ever to achieve that objective.

The increased salience of numerous troubling factors does not bode well for NATO's long-term viability. Indeed, NATO is now confronting serious threats to its future. On its 70th anniversary, the venerable alliance is showing multiple cracks and fissures. But that should not be surprising. Seven decades is a very long period for any security organization or policy to remain relevant—much less to be the optimum arrangement for dealing with new security issues. After that many decades, marked by enormous changes in European and world affairs, both the European member nations and the United States must reconsider whether NATO serves their best interests any longer. Mounting evidence indicates it does not do so for either side.

The diplomatic, economic, and security environment in Europe cries out for a new, very different, transatlantic security relationship in the 21st century. The preservation of NATO is now based more on nostalgia, mental rigidity, and the power of vested interests than on rational strategic calculations. The January 22, 2019, passage of the NATO Support Act by the House of Representatives with a 357–22 vote epitomizes such ossified thinking. That legislation bars the use of funds to facilitate in any way U.S. withdrawal from NATO. The prevailing attitude seems to be one of "NATO forever," regardless of circumstances or need.[27]

Cato Institute senior fellow Doug Bandow, a former assistant to President Ronald Reagan, aptly captures the sterile reasoning and institutional desperation that NATO partisans now exhibit. He concludes that NATO's mission seems to be little more than "to preserve itself."[28] When preserving an institution rather than adopting policies best suited to protect the republic's security has become the political elite's principal objective, that is definitive evidence of a bankrupt policy. NATO policy has reached that point, and radical change is now appropriate.

A worthwhile transatlantic security policy for the 21st century must embody two important changes based on the recognition that, although American and European security interests overlap, they are not identical. First, Washington should offload more limited and parochial challenges in Europe and its immediate neighborhood to the Europeans. The repository for such a transfer of responsibility could be either a new alliance of Europe's major powers or a European Union (EU) that becomes a security as well as an economic player in world affairs. The EU has both the population and economic resources to be such a geostrategic actor.

The United States must stop treating the prosperous and capable European nations as ineffectual security dependents.

The second needed change is to limit America's security role to problems that significantly impact important interests on both sides of the Atlantic. Insisting that all security issues be addressed through NATO is the epitome of obsolete thinking. The United States should develop a new coordinating mechanism with an independent Europeans-only entity to address security issues of mutual concern. But Washington should phase out both its military presence in Europe and, ultimately, U.S. membership in NATO. Attempting to remodel a Cold War institution to function effectively in a very different post–Cold War setting is proving frustrating and unrewarding for the United States. New thinking and a new U.S. security strategy regarding Europe have become urgent. NATO is an institutional dinosaur, and as Washington foolishly labors to expand the alliance eastward, antagonizing Russia and adding mostly small and vulnerable allies that are strategic liabilities rather than assets, it is now a dangerous dinosaur.

CHAPTER 1

NATO'S WORRISOME TRENDS AND GROWING FISSURES

As noted in the introduction, most of the traditional controversies and problems regarding NATO have involved burden sharing, with U.S. leaders demanding that the European allies boost their defense budgets and bear more of the costs of collective defense. In the 21st century, however, NATO is plagued by multiple signs of stress, divisions, and looming irrelevance. Surging anger about burden sharing is merely the most visible indication of an alliance in crisis. New thinking about NATO and its future—including whether it should even have a future—is required.

President Trump's denunciations of European free riding during the 2016 campaign and at the July 2018 NATO summit were just less-diplomatic versions of Washington's longstanding complaints. But the focus on burden sharing is unfortunate, because it obscures more fundamental problems with NATO—especially from the standpoint of U.S. interests.

Democratic Europe's attitude about its continued security dependence on the United States is starkly contradictory. On the one hand, NATO's European members seem content to spend very modest amounts on their own defense and divert financial resources to funding generous welfare states. Those countries also sometimes remain eager to offload onto the United States responsibility for dealing with security problems within and adjacent to their region. At the same time, they express increasingly pointed complaints about some U.S. policy priorities and overall U.S. arrogance.

In fairness, U.S. leaders are at least as culpable as their European counterparts for the latter's unhealthy, longtime dependency. During NATO's early years, Washington's insistence on an undisputed leadership role and democratic Europe's willingness to play a subordinate role may have been unavoidable. Time was needed for those nations to recover militarily, economically, and psychologically from the destruction and trauma of World War II.

But both Washington's paternalism and Europe's deference have persisted long after there was an arguable justification for them. As a result, the United States has undertaken defense obligations that are unnecessary, counterproductive, and often dangerous. The expansion of NATO into Eastern Europe (including into the territory of the defunct Soviet Union) to incorporate an assortment of mostly small, militarily irrelevant members vividly illustrates that phenomenon. As NATO's leader, the United States has acquired a growing roster of security dependents—some with decidedly frosty relations with their large Russian neighbor.

A policy of U.S. primacy under the rhetorical guise of "U.S. leadership" has entangled America in an assortment of unrewarding new missions. At the same time, perpetuating Washington's policy dominance into the post–Cold War era has failed to transform transatlantic security relations in a manner that could have benefited both Washington and its European allies. The way in which the NATO countries addressed the turmoil in the Balkans in the 1990s was a crucial example.

America's entanglement in the violent disintegration of Yugoslavia was unfortunate on two levels. First, it was a missed opportunity in the vastly changed post–Cold War security environment for the United States to transfer responsibility for a subregional problem to NATO's European members. Second, it transformed NATO from a defensive to an offensive alliance—and one with an expanded geographic focus. Both developments created dangerous precedents.

THE BALKAN WARS: A MISSED OPPORTUNITY FOR CONSTRUCTIVE CHANGE

As Yugoslavia began to unravel in the early 1990s, George H. W. Bush's administration initially seemed inclined to let the leading European powers manage the situation. And those powers, especially Britain, France, and Germany, did take some initiatives. For example, they tried to get the feuding ethnic factions in the newly minted country of Bosnia-Herzegovina to work out a peaceful political solution. The centerpiece of that effort, orchestrated by the EU, was the Vance-Owen plan, named for former U.S. secretary of state Cyrus Vance and former British foreign secretary David Owen.[1]

Yet even at that early stage, U.S. officials found it difficult to resist the temptation to meddle. When Bill Clinton took office, his administration spurned the Vance-Owen Plan and sent subtle signals to Bosnia's president—and the leader of the country's Muslim faction—Alija Izetbegović to resist provisions of that plan.[2] Emboldened, Izetbegović rejected the initiative, and the three-sided armed struggle among Bosnian Muslims, Croats, and Serbs intensified.

When their mediation effort faltered, European officials looked to Washington to take the lead in addressing the growing turbulence in Bosnia. U.S. officials professed reluctance to do so, but that was little more than a pro forma objection. Their activist response was fast in coming, and it reflected an underlying assumption (along with barely concealed contempt) that the Europeans were incapable of handling even modest security challenges without robust American leadership. An anonymous, high-ranking Bush administration official epitomized that attitude when he sneered, "These people could not organize a three-car motorcade if their lives depended on it."[3]

The Clinton administration not only took the policy lead, it soon dominated the process. Washington insisted that Bosnia remain intact, and U.S. policy focused on suppressing the Croat and Serb secessionist campaigns. Clinton administration officials were especially determined to thwart the bid for independence by the Republika Srpska, the Serb entity that had gained control of nearly half of Bosnia's territory and whose forces besieged the Muslim-controlled nominal national capital, Sarajevo.

Washington prodded its allies to adopt stronger anti-Serb measures, and that pressure eventually led to the first use of military force in NATO's history: the launching of air strikes against Bosnian Serb forces. The NATO intervention produced a largely dictated peace agreement, the Dayton Accords, which U.S. Assistant Secretary of State Richard Holbrooke orchestrated in November 1995.[4] Although the agreement ended the bloodshed, it did not make Bosnia anything more than a pretend country governed by a succession of international viceroys ruling through arbitrary edicts.[5] Bosnia was, and is, an economic basket case heavily dependent on international financial inputs.

Not only does the country suffer from chronic economic malaise, but deep, bitter ethnic divisions persist, making effective political cooperation nearly impossible.[6] There are signs that the ethnic animosity and divisions are growing even worse, although Western observers typically seek to blame alleged interference by Vladimir Putin instead of acknowledging the intractable societal divisions.[7] In any case, more than two decades after the civil war, Bosnia remains a dysfunctional, poverty-stricken ward of the international community. Defenders of the NATO intervention and its aftermath actually have the audacity to cite developments such as a very modest decline in the country's unemployment rate (to a still stratospheric 35.7 percent) in April 2018 as an important, positive development. They do so even though the youth unemployment rate was an even more horrific 57 percent.[8]

The Bosnia conflict was a huge missed opportunity for the United States to set new, more rational priorities for itself in the post–Cold War world. A far better policy would have been to inform the Europeans that a petty conflict in the Balkans did not reach the threshold of a serious security threat to the transatlantic community warranting direct U.S. involvement, much less requiring Washington's leadership. NATO's European members had no more right to expect a dominant U.S. role in dampening a Bosnian civil war than Americans would have had the right to expect European countries to take the lead in addressing a similar conflict in the Caribbean or Central America. By usurping the leadership role, Washington perpetuated an unhealthy European dependence—and sometimes outright free riding—on U.S. security exertions. Moreover, the U.S.-orchestrated outcome in Bosnia remains a festering political and economic mess to this day.

NATO: From Defense to Offense

Throughout the Cold War, American and European leaders consistently portrayed NATO as a purely defensive alliance. They invariably emphasized the peaceful nature of their cooperation in contrast to the Kremlin's record of belligerence and aggression. Moscow's brutal suppression of even modest political deviations within its East European satellite empire helped confirm the proclaimed difference. Soviet tanks rolled into East Germany in 1953, Hungary in 1956, and Czechoslovakia in 1968 to crush such movements. Any objective observer could clearly see that NATO was an alliance of sovereign states, while the Warsaw Pact was an imperial enterprise of puppet regimes under Moscow's total domination. Western accounts and propaganda stressed that fundamental difference, and the insistence that NATO was solely a defensive association was quite credible.

Promoting transatlantic political as well as security cooperation was, to be sure, a significant goal, and a succession of U.S. administrations encouraged greater economic and diplomatic cooperation among the democratic states of Western Europe. Washington believed that promoting such measures under the umbrella of a security organization that the United States led would discourage the renationalization of European defenses and the pursuit of narrow nationalistic policies that had caused the Continent so much grief. Yet while such objectives were relevant and significant, NATO's central purpose was to prevent any expansionist ambitions that Moscow might harbor in Europe beyond the existing satellite empire.

As time has gone on, however, NATO's image as a collection of democracies pursuing purely defensive objectives corresponds less and less to reality. Early in the post–Cold War years, the avoidance of offensive actions and objectives disappeared. The NATO interventions in Bosnia and Kosovo emphatically transformed NATO from a defensive alliance designed to deter or repel an attack on its members into an organization with an offensive orientation. In the case of Bosnia, the alliance projected military power in the midst of a civil war against a secessionist government that had not attacked or even threatened a NATO member. In the case of Kosovo, NATO used military force against a sovereign state, Serbia, recognized by the international community, to amputate one of its provinces. Once again, the target of NATO attacks had not committed the slightest act of aggression—or even threatened one—against any alliance member. Clearly, Article 5 had no applicability whatsoever to those situations.

The rationale for possible NATO military action had expanded dramatically. Citing a security justification for the interventions in the internecine Balkan conflicts flowing from Yugoslavia's breakup required a major stretch of logic. Bill Clinton's administration did assert that growing disorder in the Balkans could lead to another continent-wide crisis akin to what occurred because of the spark ignited in the region in 1914. But even most NATO partisans knew better than to emphasize such a far-fetched scenario. Instead, they focused on the alleged need to prevent a humanitarian tragedy. That justification failed to hold up to any serious scrutiny at the time, and it has grown even less credible over the years.[9]

A few NATO traditionalists were not happy about the alliance's new missions or expanded geographic focus. Writing about the Kosovo war in 1999, *Washington Post* columnist Charles Krauthammer was caustic about the increasing focus of the "new NATO" on out-of-area missions. "What was wrong with the old NATO?" he asked rhetorically. Krauthammer cited the comment of Lord Hastings Ismay, NATO's first secretary general, that NATO's purpose was to keep the Russians out, the Americans in, and the Germans down, and contended that "all three missions survive," albeit in altered, more subtle forms. "For the clever young thinkers of the [Clinton] administration," Krauthammer went on sarcastically, "this is all too boring." Referring to the transformational policies that Secretary of State Dean Acheson and other Western officials put in place after World War II, Krauthammer accused the Clinton foreign policy team of suffering from "Acheson envy" by wanting to create a memorable new international order. He saw them as trying to refashion NATO as "a robust, restless alliance ready to throw its weight around outside its own borders to impose order and goodness." The Kosovo intervention, he warned, revealed "just how unsuited" the alliance was to its new extraterritorial tasks.[10]

Krauthammer's observations were extremely perceptive. But even with his prominence in the American foreign policy community, his concerns about NATO's new focus and the dangers it posed went largely unheeded. NATO continued to become an increasingly offensive alliance with an ever-expanding out-of-area orientation.

Indeed, as transformative as the Bosnia and Kosovo interventions were, at least they occurred in Europe, a region that the NATO powers considered relevant to their security even during the Cold War. Throughout that era, the alliance (and especially the United States) maintained informal, but important, security ties to Yugoslavia during the rule of strongman Josip Broz Tito and, after his death in 1980, with his successors.[11] Washington also made it clear to Moscow that any act of military aggression against Yugoslavia would be considered a serious threat to the transatlantic community, even though the country was not a NATO member.

Now, however, many NATO military missions lie far outside the European theater. That point became evident following the September 11, 2001, terrorist attacks on the United States when Washington's NATO allies invoked Article 5. Thereafter, Germany and other alliance members sent forces to assist the U.S. military campaign in Afghanistan.

NATO's Out-of-Area Entanglements: Unwise for Europe

The new missions reflected a dramatic change in NATO's geographic coverage. It became a misnomer and distortion to regard the alliance as a "transatlantic" organization protecting the security of Europe and North America. Indeed, as the Afghanistan operation confirmed, the focus increasingly was on problems outside those two regions. That point also was evident in 2011 when the United States joined with its European allies, especially Britain and France, to launch military attacks against Libya. The ostensible purpose of the aircraft and cruise missile strikes was to thwart a bloodbath that Muammar Qaddafi's regime might unleash on innocent civilians. In reality, the intervention was another regime-change war.

The proliferation of such far-ranging missions has not been beneficial for either NATO's European members or the United States. Sending troops to Afghanistan entangled European forces in a messy, intractable war in a country that posed little threat to any of the European countries. In essence, NATO governments became junior partners in an amorphous, armed, nation-building venture that Washington was pursuing.

European leaders and their publics are showing increasing uneasiness about signing on to Washington's crusades in the Middle East and Afghanistan. Some NATO members, such as tiny Estonia, have sent token forces into Afghanistan for years in the apparent expectation that such contributions will strengthen the U.S. resolve to protect Estonia from the main threat it fears: an aggressive Russia. But entanglement in Washington's numerous wars is a very high price to pay for such an assurance.

A major reason why Islamic radicals have attacked targets in Europe is not because of a visceral hatred of Western political and cultural values—although there is some of that. The main grievance is the involvement of those countries in U.S.-led wars in the Muslim world. The perpetrators of the December 2015 attack on the Bataclan concert hall in Paris did not shout out, "This is because you let women drive!" Instead, they shouted, "This is for Syria!" France had joined with its NATO allies to back the U.S.-led war both to oust Syrian leader Bashar al-Assad and to counter the Islamic State of Iraq and Syria (ISIS), and French aircraft had been bombing ISIS-controlled areas for more than a year. The Paris attacks were bloody payback—as have been subsequent incidents in multiple NATO countries.[12]

If increasing their exposure to America's wars in the Middle East and Central Asia is now a crucial requirement of burden sharing, the Europeans would be wise to opt out. That step might or might not cause the Trump administration (or a future U.S. administration) to reconsider the rationale for the U.S. commitment to NATO. But as Washington pushes the alliance to adopt an increasingly offensive focus, and one outside of Europe, the allies could be making a major, self-destructive blunder to follow Washington's lead.

NATO's Out-of-Area Entanglements: Unwise for America

At the same time, the United States faces European calls for a more activist Western stance in Eastern Europe to deter Russia. Washington has also had to deal with calls to embark on humanitarian or regime-change military ventures in North Africa and portions of the Middle East. Responding favorably to such missions is not in the best interests of the American people. The 2011 military intervention in Libya was a textbook example of how pressure from key NATO allies, especially France and Britain, entangled America in a mission that the United States should have avoided—and without the NATO connection might have chosen to avoid.

As rebellions against authoritarian regimes erupted throughout portions of the Greater Middle East in late 2010 and early 2011 (the so-called Arab Spring), the United States and its European allies pondered how to respond. One target of an uprising was longtime Libyan dictator Muammar Qaddafi. Secretary of State Hillary Clinton described her initial reaction regarding a possible U.S.-led military intervention in the spring of 2011: "When I met with French president Nicolas Sarkozy, he urged the United States to support international military intervention to stop Qaddafi's advance toward the rebel stronghold of Benghazi in eastern Libya. I was sympathetic, but not convinced." She noted, "The United States had spent the previous decade bogged down in long and difficult wars in Iraq and Afghanistan," and she was cautious about a similar undertaking in Libya.[13]

In testimony before Congress on March 10, Clinton not only stressed the need for "international authorization" before Washington embarked on such a venture, she cited a key reason for wariness: "Too often, other countries were quick to demand action but then looked to America to shoulder all the burdens and take all the risks."[14] That comment was an unsubtle swipe at NATO's European members.

Members of the Arab League, which had long loathed the volatile Qaddafi, also were pressing for international intervention. The league included such close U.S. security partners as Saudi Arabia, Qatar, and the United Arab Emirates. But Clinton noted that, at a meeting of the Group of Eight (G-8) economic powers, "the Europeans were even more gung ho. I got an earful about military intervention from Sarkozy."[15] She was somewhat cynical about the desire of the French to flex their muscles in North Africa to gain national prestige, but similar lobbying for intervention from Britain impressed her more. "When I saw British Foreign Secretary William Hague at dinner that night, he pressed the case for action. If Hague thought military action in Libya was necessary, that counted for a lot."[16] In Clinton's opinion, Hague was a prudent pragmatist, not an impulsive crusader or someone inclined to engage in international political grandstanding.

Secretary of Defense Robert Gates also emphasized the impact of the call for military action coming from key NATO allies. Arab League lobbying "and strong British and French pressure for NATO to act, I think, together persuaded the president that the United States would need to take the lead" in organizing "a military campaign to stop Qaddafi."[17]

Following the March G-8 summit, Clinton reported to President Obama that "our NATO allies are prepared to take the lead in any military action."[18] That approach corresponded perfectly with the White House's preferences. Clinton stressed that Obama "wanted to keep U.S. involvement limited, so our allies would have to shoulder much of the burden and fly most of the sorties" that would be necessary to enforce a no-fly zone and eliminate Qaddafi's air defenses.[19]

Views among NATO's European members, though, ranged widely about how to proceed. France was so eager for the alliance to become a belligerent in Libya's civil war that Sarkozy ordered French planes into action hours before the agreed-upon time to launch the first air strikes against Qaddafi's forces. At the other extreme, Turkey agreed to the military option only with great reluctance, and NATO's most important European member, Germany, was scarcely more enthusiastic.[20] "Because we had the most capabilities," Clinton noted, "the United States started out in the lead coordinating role. The next logical step was to have NATO organize the intervention."[21]

The initial military phase certainly was overwhelmingly a U.S. operation. Navy warships in the Mediterranean launched more than 100 cruise missiles at targets in Libya. And for all the official emphasis on implementing a no-fly zone, many of those missiles were directed at Libyan ground forces advancing on rebel positions. That aspect became known as enforcing a "no-drive zone." NATO's regime-change motive, although little acknowledged, was a major factor. Indeed, Sarkozy was willing to acquiesce to Washington's demand that NATO take over official command of enforcing the no-fly zone only if France, Britain, and other willing members were allowed to aggressively pursue no-drive zone operations on their own.[22] After additional intense U.S. diplomatic efforts on that and other issues, NATO assumed formal command of the Libya military intervention, known now as Operation Unified Protector.

Even though NATO was officially in charge, the operation remained predominantly a U.S. mission. The regime-change ambitions of France, Britain, and the other European members exceeded their capabilities. Gates noted the imbalance: "All twenty-eight NATO allies voted to support the military mission in Libya, but just half provided some kind of contribution, and only eight actually provided aircraft for the strike mission. The United States had to provide the lion's share of the reconnaissance capability and most of the mid-air refueling of planes; just three months into the campaign we had to resupply even our strongest allies with precision-guided bombs and missiles—they had exhausted their meager supply. Toward the final stages, we had to reenter the fray with our own fighters and drones."[23]

It is uncertain if the United States would have launched the regime-change war in Libya without the lobbying efforts of the European allies. There were certainly influential U.S. advocates of a "humanitarian" military intervention, including within the inner circle of the Obama administration itself. Secretary of Defense Gates, an opponent of that course, cited Clinton, United Nations (UN) Ambassador Susan Rice, and senior National Security Council staffers Samantha Power and

Ben Rhodes as especially vocal proponents. But the administration was sharply divided on the issue, with Vice President Joe Biden, the chair of the Joint Chiefs of Staff, and other officials sharing Gates's reluctance.[24] The president himself seemed especially torn. Gates wrote that Obama later told him it was a very close call—a "51–49"—regarding his own views on the matter.[25]

If the administration's ambivalence was that great, pro-war input from the NATO allies may well have been the decisive factor. Without their weight on the decisionmaking scales, the Obama administration likely would have refrained from intervening in Libya. Given the disastrous outcome of that venture, such restraint would have been wise.[26] In addition to the impact of European lobbying, NATO was a useful, perhaps essential, multilateral fig leaf for the ambitions of Clinton and other pro-intervention U.S. officials. Clinton herself was quite candid about that aspect. "If there is a UN umbrella, and under that NATO is doing the operation, no one will see this as crusaders or East versus West."[27]

Equally important, no one must view the operation as a unilateral U.S. military venture. Gates noted that even though pressure for action against Qaddafi from human rights activists at home and abroad was growing in the spring of 2011, "it was clear that the president was not going to act alone or without international sanction. He wanted any military operations to be under NATO auspices."[28]

The missions in Afghanistan and Iraq (and to some extent Syria) illustrate how questionable U.S. policy preferences have dragged the European members into conflicts that they probably wished to avoid. Those interventions have brought European publics few benefits and numerous headaches. Conversely, the Libya intervention illustrates how allied pressure helped entangle the United States in a regime-change crusade that did not serve America's best interests.

The growing uneasiness evident on both sides of the Atlantic suggests a fraying consensus about NATO's proper role and greater awareness of important differences in European and American security interests. But that is not the only source of possible disunity. The rise of populism in the United States and portions of democratic Europe is producing a rebirth of foreign policy nationalism.[29] Trump's "America First" slogan is just one manifestation of that attitude. The rise of populism is leading to authoritarian policies in several NATO member countries, especially in Central and Eastern Europe, and that development has a serious potential to disrupt the alliance.

The Eroding Democratic Credentials of NATO Members

Western leaders sought from the outset to portray NATO not only as a defensive alliance, but an association of democratic states. That latter component was never entirely true, however. One founding member, Portugal, was an autocratic, quasi-fascist state under the thumb of President Antonio Salazar. When Turkey (along with Greece) joined the alliance in 1952, it was a stretch to consider that country a democracy. Although regular elections took place, and there were some protections for civil liberties and democratic norms, the Turkish military was clearly the power behind the scenes. Indeed, on two occasions, in 1960 and 1971, the armed forces took direct control of the government.

Greece also proved to be less than a stable democracy. In 1967, a cabal of colonels took over the government and ruled the country for the next seven years. In the process, the junta not only committed extensive civil liberties abuses, it triggered an intra-NATO crisis in 1974 when it orchestrated a coup against a moderate government in majority-Greek Cyprus. That maneuver led to a Turkish military intervention in Cyprus (including the seizure of nearly 40 percent of the country's territory) and nearly escalated to full-scale war between two NATO members.

The goal of deterring Soviet aggression impelled U.S. and European officials to disregard such authoritarian blemishes within the alliance. By the time the Cold War ended, though, NATO could credibly claim that it truly was an alliance of democratic nations. Even Turkey's political system seemed at least quasi-democratic, with the military's role less blatant and meddling. In recent years, however, that benign situation has changed dramatically.

Not only are fissures emerging in the alliance regarding security interests and policy preferences, but divisions regarding overall political values and practices are increasingly noticeable as well. A graphic sign of this development is the trend toward authoritarianism within several members. That source of disruption is most pronounced with respect to Turkey, but several other members are showing similar signs.

Turkey's president, Recep Tayyip Erdoğan, began exhibiting autocratic tendencies years ago. Even under the country's previous parliamentary system, when he served as prime minister, he continuously sought ways to stifle criticism and entrench his own political power. Erdoğan's crackdown on a free press and his harassment of political opponents had reached alarming levels even before the abortive July 2016 coup by elements of Turkey's military. The situation has grown much worse since that incident.

In early 2015, Steven A. Cook, a senior fellow for Middle Eastern Studies at the Council on Foreign Relations, documented the extent of Erdoğan's consolidation of power, contending that "he has become the sun around which all Turkish politics revolve." Cook noted that by then, most of the Turkish press exhibited support bordering on adoration for the prime minister and his policies, and that the dominance of that view was largely the result of "forced sales of newspapers and television stations to Erdoğan cronies." Perhaps even more unsettling than the transformation of an independent Turkish press into cogs in a partisan political machine was the media's participation in the president's growing cult of personality. Media outlets had already begun referring to Erdoğan as "Büyük Usta or Great Master." Cook noted that the atmosphere and imagery was sometimes "positively North Korean-esque."[30]

In a matter of days following the collapse of the July 2016 revolt, Erdoğan's administration not only purged hundreds of high-ranking military officers (a step for which there was at least reasonable justification) but also went after other institutions that had long impeded his attempts at autocratic rule. Nearly 3,000 judges were removed (and many of them arrested) within days of the coup attempt.[31] Erdoğan even fired 21,000 teachers from the country's school system, most because of their alleged support for his one-time ally, now staunch opponent, the religious leader Fethullah Gülen, who lives in exile in the United States.[32] The extent and speed of the systematic purge confirmed that Erdoğan simply used the attempted coup as a pretext to execute a plan already in place. Indeed, suspicions persist that the alleged revolt was a false flag operation to facilitate and legitimize the president's effort to establish a dictatorship. Erdoğan also used the episode to conduct an election changing the parliamentary system to a presidential one—with him, of course, occupying the now far more powerful post.

The purges have continued unabated since the immediate aftermath of the attempted coup, as have ever more repressive measures. Criticism of the regime or its policies is now extremely muted. Today, Erdoğan's Turkey more closely resembles Putin's Russia than a genuine Western democracy.

Erdoğan's political party has won every election since 2000, including the most recent one in June 2018. Serious questions remain about that apparent political mandate, however. Not the least of them is the timing of the 2018 balloting: it was a snap election that Erdoğan called to solidify his power, with the all of the ongoing "state of emergency" restrictions imposed after the 2016 coup attempt still in place. Other questions emerged about voter intimidation, the security of ballots, and the accuracy of the vote count. Those concerns also existed with the April 2017 referendum that changed Turkey's government from a parliamentary to a presidential system.[33] The bottom line was that the entire election process in both 2017 and 2018 was neither free nor fair.[34] The president and his political allies controlled nearly all of the main information sources, especially radio and television outlets.[35] During the final days before the elections, only Erdoğan had television access to voters.[36]

Among NATO member countries, authoritarian trends are the most pronounced in Turkey, but that country is hardly the only one exhibiting that disturbing trait.[37] U.S. and European leaders express growing concern about the authoritarianism enveloping Hungarian prime minister Viktor Orbán's government. In a September 2014 speech, President Obama sharply criticized various regimes around the world for undermining civil institutions and engaging in various forms of repression. Most of his targets, including China, Venezuela, and Egypt, were predictable, since they were indisputably authoritarian political systems. But the president also included NATO and EU member Hungary among the nations in which "endless regulations and overt intimidation increasingly target civil society."[38]

Hungary has not yet traveled quite as far as Turkey down the path of autocracy, but the trend is noticeable. Orbán has shown a disturbing intolerance of critics, including a willingness to harass them. Exploiting the unprecedented electoral success of his governing party, Fidesz, which amassed a super majority in parliament following elections in 2010,[39] the prime minister pursued various initiatives to consolidate power. One key development was the successful campaign in 2013 to enact major constitutional changes—including measures that Hungary's highest court had previously ruled unconstitutional, which weakened legislative and judicial checks on the prime minister's authority.[40]

Even before the passage of those amendments, Orbán's administration had initiated a crackdown reminiscent of those Erdoğan and Putin waged on media critics and human rights activists. The remaining independent journalists felt increasingly menaced. At one point, Orbán even proposed mandatory drug testing for journalists.[41] One of the prime minister's biggest targets was the Hungarian Civil Liberties Union, which has led a campaign to oppose his efforts to constrain freedom of expression and undermine dissidents. Using rhetoric reminiscent of Putin, he asserted that such groups are "paid political activists attempting to assert foreign interests in Hungary."

Orbán's war on foreign nongovernmental organizations continues to intensify. In late 2018, the government even ordered the closure of the Central European University.[42] Billionaire Hungarian-American financier George Soros had founded that institution, and he remained its principal funder. He also had become an outspoken critic of Viktor Orbán and his policies. Orbán's vitriol against Soros was steadily escalating even before the closure of the university. Such a drastic action, though, sent a blunt message to advocates of democracy in Hungary—and to their foreign backers.

Orbán's authoritarian and xenophobic impulses have been worsening at a brisk pace. In one interview, he reportedly denounced the entire concept of multiculturalism and asserted that there should be no "mass scale" intermixing of different creeds.[43] The government's foreign and national security policies reflect that stance. As early as 2015, Hungary defied Brussels and unilaterally suspended application of the European Union's asylum policy, contending that Hungary's culture was being overwhelmed by an influx of refugees, primarily from the Middle East and North Africa. In March 2017, another new law went into effect empowering authorities to hold children as well as adult refugees in "containment camps" just inside the border.[44]

Hungary's European partners in both NATO and the EU have expressed alarm about the political developments in that country.[45] U.S. policymakers and journalists are showing similar concern and agitation. A CNN news story in April 2018 concluded darkly that "space for civil society and a functional independent media in Hungary is shrinking rapidly."[46] The expanded crackdown on Soros-funded organizations illustrates the repressive atmosphere and the Orbán administration's hostility toward civil society activism.

Poland is the latest addition to the roster of NATO countries drifting—or rushing—toward autocracy. The electoral victory of the right-wing Law and Justice Party (known by its Polish acronym PiS) in October 2015 ushered in a number of troubling developments. The new government promptly pardoned the notorious head of the country's security services, who had received a prison sentence for various abuses of power. But most alarming, the PiS regime ignored several rulings of Poland's Constitutional Tribunal. One of the rulings invalidated the government's attempt to replace five justices with new appointees. The prime minister and his colleagues defied the court and seated the new justices anyway. It was a brazen maneuver that surpassed President Franklin D. Roosevelt's notorious court-packing scheme and would have made even that renowned player of political hardball blush.

The initial Polish power play alarmed both domestic critics and EU officials. Some 50,000 people poured into the streets of Warsaw in December 2015 to "defend democracy," and Andrzej Zoll, former president of the Constitutional Tribunal, warned that "twenty-five years of democratic Poland are coming to an end."[47] EU Parliament president Martin Schulz described the actions of the Polish government as amounting to a "coup."[48]

The situation has steadily worsened over the past three years. In the summer of 2018, the PiS administration expanded the rationale it had used to pack the Constitutional Tribunal to transform the rest of the judiciary politically and ideologically. It mandated the retirement of all judges over age 65—unless the government explicitly exempted a judge. Ruling party officials asserted that such a step was necessary to eliminate jurists from the communist era, but Brian Porter-Szucs, professor of history at the University of Michigan, points out that "only a few hundred judges out of around 10,000 began their careers on the bench prior to the fall of communism in 1989. Those judges were long ago screened to weed out those who had issued politically motivated rulings."[49] Porter-Szucs notes that some 40 percent of judges would be forced out of office and replaced by regime loyalists. This step, he contends, amounts to "a political takeover of the independent Polish judiciary."[50]

Poland is now showing unmistakable signs of following Turkey and Hungary far down the path toward autocracy. Those trends are not confined to undermining judicial independence, although that is an especially alarming development. On Poland's Independence Day in November 2017, more than 60,000 pro-government marchers filled Warsaw's streets, chanting "pure Poland, white Poland," in an emphatic and clearly racist opposition to immigration. The minister of the interior later called it "a beautiful sight."[51] University of Texas scholar Molly O'Neal also points out that PiS leaders seem increasingly fond of the highly autocratic leader of Poland during the years between the two world wars, Józef Piłsudski. The public nostalgia for Piłsudski is clearly evident—and growing—among PiS supporters as well.[52]

The surge of populist nationalism in Poland, displacing the more liberal "civic nationalism," may pose a greater challenge to the values-driven EU than the security-oriented NATO, but it creates problems for both institutions. O'Neal notes that not only are the PiS government and its followers hostile to the EU and its cosmopolitan values, but they are especially resentful toward the EU's leading power, Germany.[53] Historical grievances contribute to that attitude. But playing an even greater role seems to be the sense that Berlin is a key source of perceived EU interference in Poland's internal affairs aimed at undermining the country's national identity and promoting cosmopolitanism.

One consequence of the growing anti-German perspective is that Warsaw wants closer ties (especially military ties) with the United States to guard against a Russian resurgence, but looser ties with Germany and the EU. Not only does that dynamic foster an intensified, unhealthy security dependence on Washington, but it undermines efforts to create a greater EU security role. The PiS regime and its supporters apparently favor the status quo of basing Poland's security on a U.S.-dominated NATO rather than a French-German-led European security arrangement. But while Washington apparently can rely on Poland to be an enthusiastic security ally, U.S. leaders may have to confront the troubling reality that America is in an awkward relationship with an increasingly authoritarian ally.

What we are witnessing in Hungary and Poland is just an extreme version of an authoritarian populist trend that is transforming much of Central and Eastern Europe. Writing in *Foreign Affairs,* Ivan Krastev, chair of the Centre for Liberal Strategies in Sofia, Bulgaria, describes the phenomenon as an "illiberal revolution."[54] That may be a bit of an overstatement, but the political and ideological trends in the region are troubling. America is at risk of being obligated to defend an array of undemocratic, even downright repressive, NATO allies.

Growing Friction over Political Values and Security Perspectives

Mounting uneasiness and even anger about the autocratic behavior of Turkey and some of the newer partners—especially Hungary and Poland—is evident in the United States and various other Cold War–era NATO countries. Critics are becoming quite vocal. American Enterprise Institute scholar Dalibor Rohac, for example, asserts flatly that Hungary and Poland are no longer democratic.[55]

Indeed, a growing chorus of critics is calling for the outright expulsion of Turkey, given the Erdoğan government's brazen authoritarianism and other sins.[56] Their complaints cite both Ankara's repressive governance and Erdoğan's increasingly cozy relationship with Moscow. The most visible symbol of that cooperation was the $2.5 billion sale of Russian S-400 air defense missiles to Turkey negotiated in December 2017.[57] When reports of an impending deal surfaced in the autumn of 2017, the United States and other NATO members expressed their unhappiness, not only because those weapons cannot be integrated into NATO's overall air defenses, but because such a deal symbolized the extent of Turkish-Russian collaboration. Indeed, alliance officials warned Ankara of negative "consequences" for going ahead with the agreement.[58]

The bilateral collaboration now goes far beyond the missile issue. The two governments (along with U.S. arch-adversary Iran) signed an oil and gas drilling agreement in August 2017. The measure followed a 2016 deal to build a Black Sea gas pipeline that bypassed Ukraine.[59] Such steps are hardly consistent with Washington's (or NATO's) policy of imposing sanctions on Russia for the Kremlin's annexation of Crimea and support for separatist forces in eastern Ukraine. Indeed, Ankara opposes the entire Western sanctions strategy against Moscow.[60]

The alliance will likely find it far more difficult in the 21st century than during the Cold War to look the other way if a member succumbs to dictatorial impulses. Even as vocal a NATO-phile as Celeste Wallander concedes, "After the fall of the Soviet Union, the liberal democratic credentials became even more important to the alliance." NATO "sought to leverage the desire for membership to encourage political reforms by requiring that new members meet its standards for good governance."[61] She is worried about the political trends, especially in Central and Eastern Europe, and that NATO's political strategy may be failing.

During the Cold War, NATO was widely understood to be primarily an anti-Soviet defense association. The professed commitment to liberal democracy, while important, was secondary. But in the post–Cold War era, NATO leaders repeatedly have stressed the organization's commitment to democracy and human rights. Having Putin-style autocracies in NATO's ranks would be more than a little embarrassing. Yet that is now a worry with respect to multiple members, especially Poland, Hungary, and Turkey. Indeed, in the last case, calling that country a democracy is already a cynical misnomer.

Multiplying Fissures Plague NATO

NATO now faces severe stresses and fissures on the level of values as well as security needs and preferences.[62] Moreover, both sets of problems are clearly getting worse, not better. In some cases, the strands of dissent and disunity seem to feed into one another, although that is not always true. Poland's populist-authoritarian government favors a hard line toward Russia, fearing a renewed security threat from Moscow. But Hungary clearly does not, and the trend in Turkey is toward accommodation, not confrontation. The populist-inclined coalition that took power in Italy in 2018 is exhibiting similar tendencies. In October, the country's deputy prime minister stated bluntly that Rome would oppose the renewal of EU sanctions against Russia.[63]

A fraying consensus about security policy combined with the sharp erosion of democratic values among several NATO members underscores the need for the United States to reconsider its NATO policy and downsize its European defense commitments. It is bad enough for U.S. leaders to risk the lives of the American people to defend a liberal democratic ally when that ally is not essential to the security of the republic. It is much worse to incur such a risk to defend a thinly disguised dictatorship that is not essential to America's security. And it is still worse when such a supposed ally cannot be relied upon to support U.S. foreign policy objectives. Yet that is the ugly combination we face already with Turkey—and we confront multiple signs of similarly unpalatable developments in other NATO countries.

The proliferating problems plaguing NATO cannot be papered over by invoking vapid clichés about everlasting alliance solidarity.[64] Policy change has now become essential and perhaps unavoidable. Washington needs to adopt a much more cautious and selective security relationship with the European powers. Unfortunately, the conventional wisdom in the United States seems to be that enlarging NATO and having the alliance pursue an ever-widening list of offensive goals in Europe and other regions is the appropriate strategy.

Especially disheartening is the apparent determination of America's political and policy elites to wage a new cold war with Russia. Such a course will make relations with that nuclear-armed power needlessly tense and dangerous. Indeed, to a large extent, it has already done so.

CHAPTER 2

FATEFUL DECISION: NATO EXPANSION AND THE ROAD TO A NEW COLD WAR

During the first decade and a half of the post–Cold War era, NATO changed from a defensive to an offensive—or at least a hybrid defensive-offensive—alliance. It conducted combat operations for the first time—and did so outside of its traditional territory, both in the Balkans and in Afghanistan. Equally significant, NATO expanded its coverage into Central and Eastern Europe by adding numerous new members. The combination of those changes gradually poisoned relations with Russia.

Most Americans and other Westerners appear to have difficulty comprehending how much U.S.-NATO policy created tensions with Moscow and put both sides onto the path of a second cold war. Yet Washington bears much of the responsibility for that alarming outcome. Indeed, some of the damage occurred well before Vladimir Putin became Russia's president and set democratic Russia on a more authoritarian course. Former U.S. ambassador to the Soviet Union Jack F. Matlock Jr. cites the negative impact of NATO expansion and the U.S.-led military interventions in the Balkans on Russian attitudes toward the United States and the West:

> President Bill Clinton supported NATO's bombing of Serbia without U.N. Security Council approval and the expansion of NATO to include former Warsaw Pact countries. Those moves seemed to violate

> the understanding that the United States would not take advantage of the Soviet retreat from Eastern Europe. The effect on Russians' trust in the United States was devastating. In 1991, polls indicated that about 80 percent of Russian citizens had a favorable view of the United States; in 1999, nearly the same percentage had an unfavorable view.[1]

In retrospect, what is surprising is just how accommodating the Kremlin seemed to be during the final years of the Cold War and the initial post–Cold War years. John Mearsheimer, the R. Wendell Harrison Distinguished Service Professor of Political Science at the University of Chicago, notes the mildness of Moscow's views on NATO: "When the Cold War was ending, the Soviet Union made it clear that it favored keeping the U.S. military in Europe and maintaining NATO. The Soviet leaders understood that this arrangement had kept Germany pacified since World War II and would continue doing so after the country reunified and became much more powerful."[2] The Russians seemed to subscribe to the portions of NATO Secretary General Lord Ismay's admonition about keeping the Americans in and the Germans down.

The issue of a united Germany in NATO was more contentious. In his memoirs, James A. Baker III, George H. W. Bush's secretary of state, describes how Soviet leaders at first were strongly opposed to German membership in NATO if the country was reunified. However, they were equally uneasy about a united Germany outside the alliance. Although Soviet leader Mikhail Gorbachev and Foreign Minister Eduard Shevardnadze toyed with the latter idea, they worried about such a powerful entity operating entirely on its own without the institutional restraints that the United States and the other leading NATO members could impose.

Bush and his national security adviser, Brent Scowcroft, confirm how reluctant the Soviet leaders were initially about even the prospect of a united Germany, much less a united Germany in NATO. They describe how Gorbachev gradually, and grudgingly, came to accept that outcome.[3] Baker and other Bush administration officials made a concerted effort to convince Gorbachev and Shevardnadze that a united

Germany would be less dangerous embedded in NATO than operating as an independent, "nonaligned" power. Baker concedes, though, that it was not an easy sell.[4]

Indeed, it was not. Bush recalls telling Gorbachev that "given history, Germany in NATO—coupled with a stabilizing U.S. presence through the alliance—was best for everyone." The answer to his concerns, Bush insisted, "was to change the nature of NATO."[5] To facilitate the prospects of Moscow's acceptance, Washington's diplomatic rationale emphasized that with the ending of acute East-West tensions, NATO already was changing in fundamental ways, especially by increasing the emphasis on a political rather than a military role. Bush and Scowcroft recalled that "if we were to have any chance" of convincing the Soviets to accept a united Germany in NATO "we would have to demonstrate how the character of the alliance was changing."[6]

Gorbachev, though, remained somewhat skeptical about such assurances, and Shevardnadze even more so. At one point in the discussions, Gorbachev noted that U.S. leaders intended to retain the Western political-military bloc, even as the Soviet bloc clearly was dissolving. Such a position in his view seemed to contradict the goal of a new, much more cordial East-West relationship. He also seemed to test some of the core U.S. assurances, musing at one point, "I will say to the President that we want to enter NATO. After all, you said that NATO wasn't directed against us, you said it was a new Europe, so why shouldn't we apply?"[7] Not surprisingly, Baker and other officials tried to move the discussion past that query as quickly as possible.

NATO preservation, including the addition of a united Germany and the continued deployment of U.S. military forces on the Continent was one thing; the Soviets ultimately were willing, albeit with reluctance, to accept such a result. Expanding the alliance beyond a united Germany was an entirely different matter as far as the Soviet Union (and later, Russia) was concerned. Indeed, there was some division and uneasiness within NATO itself about the alliance incorporating even a united Germany. British prime minister Margaret Thatcher expressed reservations about German reunification and even more concerns about moving NATO military forces into what would become the former East German state. Noting that with that step, "NATO would be moving [east]," and that the development was likely to make Gorbachev uneasy, Thatcher insisted: "He's got to be given some reassurance." Scowcroft admits that he was "dismayed" that Thatcher was essentially advocating "a demilitarized East Germany."[8]

Bush administration officials were exceedingly pleased about the ultimate results of their diplomatic handiwork in getting Soviet acceptance of a united Germany in NATO. Scowcroft stated later that the outcome was one "in which there were only winners." The administration, he contends, worked very hard "to move alliance strategy away from the Soviet Union and toward post–Cold War objectives. This gave Gorbachev the opportunity to argue to his Politburo that NATO had been transformed and was no longer a threat." And such a perception was correct, he insists. "We had moved ahead the transformation of NATO, establishing its direction to act as a political instrument of European stabilization rather than one of military confrontation."[9]

Perhaps Scowcroft genuinely believed that benign narrative. But even in his account, an undertone suggests the presence of different, more self-serving U.S. intentions. He expresses great satisfaction that the Warsaw Pact had formally dissolved. "I believed that NATO alone would retain an important role in European security and stability, and the U.S. with it."[10] Preserving Washington's hegemonic position in Europe seemed to be more than a minor consideration.

President Bush's attitude certainly did not reflect a "there were only winners" perspective. His candid comments during a session with West German chancellor Helmut Kohl clearly suggest a different view. Regarding the Soviet position against a united Germany staying in NATO, Bush erupted: "To hell with that! *We prevailed, they didn't. We can't let the Soviets clutch victory from the jaws of defeat.*"[11] That certainly seems like the attitude of a triumphant victor, not someone who believed in reconciliation and "only winners" in ending the Cold War. Indeed, the United States behaved as typical hegemonic powers—or rising powers exploiting declining ones—have done throughout history.[12]

NATO Encroaches on a Democratic Russia

The results have been most unfortunate, and plenty of warning signs of trouble were evident as Washington increasingly pressed its advantage. Mearsheimer concludes that even in the early 1990s, "Moscow was deeply opposed to NATO enlargement. The Russians believed their Western counterparts understood their fears and the alliance would not expand" eastward beyond Germany. Unfortunately, "the Clinton administration thought otherwise and in the 1990s began pushing NATO expansion."[13]

The belief that NATO would not move farther eastward was a key reason why Gorbachev and Shevardnadze were willing, however reluctantly, to countenance not only a united Germany, but a united Germany within NATO. In his memoirs, Baker skirts around the issue of U.S. and Western assurances to the Kremlin regarding NATO's ambitions beyond membership for Germany following reunification. But it is difficult to imagine any Soviet leader acquiescing to an open-ended enlargement of the alliance. Indeed, the bulk of the evidence indicates that U.S. officials did offer at least implicit promises to the contrary (more on this below).

Moves toward NATO expansion (or "enlargement"—the euphemism its advocates preferred) soon generated Russian suspicions and apprehension. Even a staunch expansion proponent such as Strobe Talbott, deputy secretary of state in Bill Clinton's administration, acknowledged that effect:

> One of the most difficult challenges to enlarging NATO is its effect on Russia. Many Russians see NATO as a vestige of the cold war, inherently directed against their country. They point out that they have disbanded the Warsaw Pact, *their* military alliance, and ask why the West should not do the same. For them, NATO's plan to take in new members looks like a Western vote of no-confidence in the staying power of Russian reform. It makes them feel as though Russia is still on probation—still subject to a thinly disguised policy of containment. . . . These suspicions and warnings reverberate across the Russian political spectrum. They are exploited by conservative, reactionary, and fascistic elements who use the prospect of enlarging NATO as proof that the West is bent on humiliating Russia, keeping it weak, plotting its demise.[14]

Despite such indications that NATO expansion would create a hostile reaction in Russia, the Clinton administration remained determined to push expansion. Indeed, the new administration had adopted that goal privately within its first few months—although it continued to be coy on the issue for a while in its public statements. In her memoirs, Madeleine Albright, who served as U.S. ambassador to the United Nations (UN) and later as secretary of state, confirmed that the actual decision was made in June 1993. "We believed that NATO had to remain at the center of the European security system. No other institution had comparable clout. Second, it was only fair that NATO should open its doors to the new democracies, provided they met the same political and military standards as other members." The administration, she stated, did conclude that "enlargement should occur gradually," rather than abruptly. Although the meaning of "gradually" was not clear, the ultimate objective was never in doubt.[15]

Talbott's speech was just one of several major addresses in 1995 by high-level officials confirming that the administration already was determined to begin implementing its goal of expanding the alliance. Secretary of State Warren Christopher and UN Ambassador Albright also made prominent contributions to the pro-expansion rhetorical barrage.[16]

Even the first stage of expansion in 1998, which offered membership to Poland, Hungary, and the Czech Republic, annoyed Russia and fueled Moscow's suspicions about long-term U.S. intentions in Eastern Europe. With regard to that first proposed round, Albright concedes, "[President Boris] Yeltsin and his countrymen were strongly opposed to enlargement, seeing it as a strategy for exploiting their vulnerability and moving Europe's dividing line to the east, leaving them isolated."[17] She and other advocates of admitting Central and East European members insist that the Russian perception was wrong. The goal of both Washington and the newly free European countries, she insists, "was to do for Europe's East what NATO and the Marshall Plan had done for Europe's West. Their goal was to create a sphere of common interest in which every nation would live in security."[18]

Republican proponents of expansion expressed similar views. Looking back on her years in George W. Bush's administration, Condoleezza Rice contends that "NATO had become a vital instrument in the stabilization of post-communist Europe. Together with the European Union, it gave aspirant states from the former Eastern bloc a lodestar as they sought to reform and to end old rivalries between them. This was a replay of NATO's original mission at the end of World War II. Although many remembered the Alliance principally as a barrier to Russian [sic] expansion, there had been a second purpose: NATO's founders saw it as a democratic umbrella under which old rivals could resolve their differences." Rice admits, though, that replicating that mission in Central and Eastern Europe, "required the continuous expansion of the Alliance."[19] It is especially unsettling that Rice, considered an expert on the Soviet Union and Russia, would not only regard the Cold War era as marked by Russian (not Soviet) expansion, but that she seemed oblivious or unconcerned about how Russians would view the expansion of a powerful Western military alliance right up to the borders of their country.

Even if Rice and other "Atlanticists" actually believed the rationale of spreading stability and democracy rather than simply mouthing it, the West's moves did not allay Moscow's concerns. Token gestures of conciliation—such as creating a liaison mechanism in the NATO-Russia Founding Act and allowing Russian officials to participate in NATO meetings—did not resolve that problem. Moreover, NATO's moves to expand undermined the credibility of pro-Western members of Russia's leadership elite. They had relied upon the informal assurances that if the Kremlin acquiesced to a united Germany in NATO, the alliance would not expand beyond Germany's eastern border. They relayed such assurances to the Russian people, ultimately discrediting themselves politically.

In a 2009 interview with *Der Spiegel*, then–Russian president Dmitry Medvedev typified the bitterness of Russian leaders. Medvedev complained that after the Berlin Wall came down, it had "not been possible to redefine Russia's place in Europe." Moscow's main hope was for a true European-wide security arrangement, either through the creation of a new organization or through a more empowered Organization for Security and Cooperation in Europe. What did Russia get instead? "None of the things that we were assured, namely that NATO would not expand endlessly eastwards and our interests would be continuously taken into consideration."[20]

U.S. officials and their defenders among American foreign policy academics vehemently dispute that contention. In a 2009 *Washington Quarterly* article, Mark Kramer, a scholar at Harvard University's Davis Center for Russian and Eurasian Studies, even asserted that such claims were a complete myth. "Indeed," he insisted, "the issue [of NATO expansion beyond East Germany] never came up during the negotiations on German reunification."[21] Mary Elise Sarotte, Dean's Professor of History at the University of Southern California, effectively debunks that argument, providing evidence that the issue arose "soon after the Berlin Wall opened" and was discussed several times. However, she also concludes that "there was never a formal deal, as Russia alleges. . . ."[22]

The United States correctly asserts that nothing was put in writing affirming a geographic limitation on NATO's membership; however, the clarity, extent, and duration of any verbal commitment to refrain from expansion remain matters of intense controversy.[23] And invoking the "you didn't get it in writing" dodge did not inspire the Kremlin's trust. Indeed, media and scholarly critics of NATO's expansion argue that the United States and its NATO allies clearly misled the Kremlin.

Documents unearthed from various national archives in the past two years tend to support the contention that U.S. and Western officials gave at least implied assurances about NATO having no expansionist ambitions east of Germany.[24] Svetlana Savranskaya and Tom Blanton, analysts at the National Security archive, examined those documents and concluded "that discussions of NATO in the context of German unification negotiations in 1990 were not at all narrowly limited to the status of East German territory, and that subsequent Soviet and Russian complaints about being misled about NATO expansion were founded in written contemporaneous memcons [memos of face-to-face conversations] and telcons [memos of telephone conversations] at the highest levels."[25]

The initial round of enlargement, combined with the West's brazen military interventions in the Balkans, undermined friendly relations with Russia. NATO partisans deny this and argue that the deterioration of East-West relations did not really commence until Russia launched its war against Georgia in 2008. Some even contend that a major breakdown did not take place until Russia seized Crimea and intervened in eastern Ukraine to support secessionist forces in 2014.[26]

Such arguments are inaccurate at best and utterly disingenuous at worst. George Kennan, the intellectual father of America's containment policy during the Cold War, perceptively warned in a May 2, 1998, *New York Times* interview what the Senate's ratification of NATO's first round of expansion would set in motion. "I think it is the beginning of a new cold war," Kennan stated. "I think the Russians will gradually react quite adversely and it will affect their policies. I think it is a tragic mistake. There was no reason for this whatsoever. No one was threatening anybody else. This expansion would make the Founding Fathers of this country turn over in their graves."[27]

Mearsheimer observes correctly that, with regard to NATO's move east, "Russian leaders complained bitterly from the start."[28] President Clinton conceded as much. He asserted that his goal was to "establish a process for opening NATO's door to the Central European nations in a way that wouldn't cause Yeltsin too many problems in Russia." The vehicle for that, Clinton believed, was the Partnership for Peace—a halfway house toward full NATO membership for those countries.

But Yeltsin was not happy with U.S. policy regarding NATO. In a December 1994 speech, he accused Clinton of trading a cold war for a "cold peace" by pushing NATO expansion. Clinton was miffed. "I was stunned and angry, because I didn't know what had set him off."[29] The president's cluelessness continued during the following years. When the Russian leader gave a tough speech at the UN General Assembly in October 1995, Clinton dismissed it as "mostly for domestic consumption," and concluded that Yeltsin was under a lot of pressure at home "from ultranationalists over NATO expansion and the aggressive role the United States was playing in Bosnia."[30]

The inability of Clinton and other U.S. officials to recognize the mounting warning signals coming out of Moscow is breathtaking. Shortly after Yeltsin's reelection in 1996, Clinton met with him in Helsinki. Clinton's account of the meeting epitomized the tone-deaf nature of U.S. policy regarding NATO expansion. "When I told Boris that I wanted NATO both to expand and to sign an agreement with

Russia, he asked me to commit secretly—in his words 'in a closet'—to limiting future NATO expansion to the Warsaw Pact, thus excluding the states of the former Soviet Union, like the Baltics and Ukraine." That initiative constituted a considerable dilution of the position that Gorbachev and Shevardnadze had pushed—no alliance expansion beyond the eastern border of a united Germany.

Yet Clinton utterly spurned the compromise offer. "I said I couldn't do that because, first of all, it wouldn't remain secret, and doing so would undermine the credibility of the Partnership for Peace." He then told Yeltsin that such a limitation would not be "in America's or Russia's interest. NATO's governing mission is no longer directed against Russia but against the new threats to peace and stability in Europe." Despite that assurance, he notes, "Yeltsin was still afraid of the domestic reaction to expansion."[31]

My own interactions with Russian diplomats, academics, and journalists during the mid- and late-1990s confirm that the negative attitude about Washington's increasingly apparent desire to expand NATO eastward was not confined to Russia's political elite. Uniformly, they expressed anger and feelings of betrayal. However, Russia was too weak militarily and economically to do anything about the U.S.-led intrusion.

As former ambassador Jack Matlock points out, NATO's conduct in the unraveling Yugoslavia reinforced Russia's fears about the consequences for their immediate neighborhood if the alliance continued moving eastward. That point was apparent as early as 1995 when NATO planes began bombing Serb positions during Bosnia's civil war. Yeltsin responded that "this is the first sign of what could happen when NATO comes right up to the Russian Federation's borders."[32] Moscow's trust in Western intentions was fading markedly and fast.

The second round of expansion in 2004 brought into NATO not only more former Warsaw Pact members, but the Baltic republics, entities that had been part of the Soviet Union itself. Moreover, George W. Bush's administration made clear that the United States intended to see the alliance add both Georgia and Ukraine in yet another round of enlargement. Bush enthusiastically embraced the ambitions of both countries for membership and strongly lobbied for that goal.[33]

Washington's European allies began to balk, however. France, Germany, and other long-standing alliance partners were unwilling to support that step when Bush formally proposed the first stage in the admission process, a Membership Action Plan, for Georgia and Ukraine at the April 2008 NATO summit in Bucharest, Romania.[34] Secretary of State Rice recalls that German chancellor Angela Merkel was especially negative. Merkel "did not trust the Georgians, whom she still saw as corrupt." The German leader also observed that Ukraine's governing coalition following the 2004 Orange Revolution "was a mess."[35]

Although the primary reason for Western European reluctance was the unsatisfactory domestic political and economic situations in both countries, there also was uneasiness that another round of NATO expansion might fatally damage already delicate relations with Russia. Even Bush concedes that officials in both Paris and Berlin were worried about that aspect, noting that "Angela Merkel and Nicolas Sarkozy . . . were skeptical. They knew Georgia and Ukraine had tense relationships with Moscow, and they worried NATO could get drawn into a war with Russia."[36]

Despite the intra-alliance resistance to the Bush administration's push to offer Membership Action Plans to Kiev and Tbilisi, the outcome of the Bucharest summit was not a total defeat for U.S. ambitions. The summit's final declaration contained language stating, "NATO welcomes Ukraine's and Georgia's Euro Atlantic aspirations for membership in NATO. We agreed today that these countries will become members of NATO."[37] No timetable was given, but the ultimate outcome seemed clear.

The Kremlin's anger threatened to boil over at this point, and Moscow began to push back. Even before the final summit declaration, Vladimir Putin bluntly warned alliance members, "The emergence of a powerful military bloc at our borders will be seen as a direct threat to Russian security."[38] The country's deputy foreign minister, Alexander Grushko, stated that NATO membership for Georgia and Ukraine would be "a huge strategic mistake" causing the "most serious consequences" for European peace and security.[39]

Germany, France, and other key European allies became even more wary of provoking the Kremlin by adding Georgia and Ukraine to

NATO when war broke out between Georgia and Russia in August 2008 (see Chapter 4). Initial European condemnations of Russian aggression began to fade as evidence emerged that Tbilisi had made the first military move in the crisis. The reluctance of "old Europe" (Secretary of Defense Donald Rumsfeld's dismissive label) to support NATO membership for Georgia and Ukraine has diminished little since that time.

Unfortunately, neither has Washington's determination to see those countries admitted to NATO. Even the persistence of severe tensions between Russia and Ukraine since the 2014 crisis has had little sobering effect on Washington. During a visit to Tbilisi in August 2017, Vice President Mike Pence blithely declared, "President Trump and I stand by the 2008 NATO Bucharest statement, which made it clear that Georgia will one day become a member of NATO." He added, "We strongly support Georgia's aspiration to become a member of NATO. And we'll continue to work closely with this Prime Minister and the government of Georgia broadly to advance the policies that will facilitate becoming a NATO member."[40]

Indeed, American anti-Russian hawks seem more determined than ever to extend Washington's security umbrella over Ukraine and Georgia. Writing in the *Weekly Standard* in 2014, former UN ambassador (and later national security adviser) John Bolton made that objective clear:

> Obama left Ukraine and Georgia to fend for themselves, ignoring the politico-military reality that Russia instinctively understood. He thereby left open the vulnerability that Bush had tried to close in April 2008. Many who now oppose robust U.S. efforts to protect Ukraine from Russian depredation and partition assert that we have no serious interests there, and accordingly also reject any hint we might once again consider NATO membership. Yet, in the long term, joining the alliance is the only strategy that can realistically secure Georgian and Ukrainian sovereignty and keep alive the option of joining the West more broadly.[41]

That position was a bit much even for a renowned hawkish Russophobe like former national security adviser Zbigniew Brzezinski. Although he favored sending arms to Ukraine, he drew the line at giving Kiev NATO membership, recognizing what a severe provocation it would be to Russia. Writing in the *American Interest*, he stated that "there should be clarity that Ukraine will not be a member of NATO. I think that is important for a variety of political reasons. If you look at the map, it's important for Russia from a psychological, strategic point of view." Brzezinski even believed that Putin would be receptive to Ukraine joining the EU, if it was clear that NATO membership would not follow.[42]

Other members of the American foreign policy community want to push ahead on the latter goal, however. Luke Coffey, director of the Douglas and Sarah Allison Center for Foreign Policy at the conservative Heritage Foundation, issued a report in January 2018 titled "NATO Membership for Georgia: In U.S. and European Interest." In the report, Coffey states flatly that the United States must "continue to be an advocate for Georgia's eventual membership in NATO." The report also urged NATO members at the July 2018 summit in Brussels to reaffirm the commitment originally made in 2008 concerning eventual membership for Georgia.[43]

Continuing enthusiasm for adding Georgia and Ukraine to NATO is not confined to conservative or neoconservative precincts. Damon Wilson and David J. Kramer, scholars at the Atlantic Council, authored an August 2018 report, "Enlarge NATO to Ensure Peace in Europe." They argue, "Extending NATO membership to nations who earn it can eliminate destabilizing security vacuums." In their view, not taking such a step creates needless dangers. "Without a sense of timing on when such membership is coming, the dangerous gray zone that Ukraine and Georgia find themselves in will continue. Allies should not allow their aspirations to be held hostage by Russian occupation.[44]

Delusional Thinking or Arrogance? Washington's Motives for NATO Expansion

Washington's never-ending quest to expand NATO seemed calculated to emphasize that Russia had lost the Cold War and should, therefore, be content with the role of a defeated, second-tier power. That attitude and the policies it spawned poisoned East-West relations and created the conditions for a second cold war.

U.S. officials insisted, however, that NATO expansion was not directed at Russia and that Russian officials should not consider the process hostile or menacing. Quite the contrary, they maintained. Strobe Talbott argued that embedding Eastern Europe's newly liberated nations in both the EU and NATO was the key to future stability in the region. Enlargement of NATO, he predicted, "would be a force for the rule of law within Europe's new democracies and among them."[45] Promoting such stability, the argument went, actually would benefit Russia.

However, Talbott (and other Clinton administration officials) clearly considered Russia to be in a separate, decidedly less trustworthy, category than other nations in Eastern Europe:

> First, NATO is and will remain for the foreseeable future, including when it takes in new members, a military alliance and a collective defense pact. Second, among the contingencies for which NATO must be prepared is that Russia will abandon democracy and return to the threatening patterns of international behavior that have sometimes characterized its history, particularly during the Soviet period. Uncertainty about Russia's future is inescapably among the factors to be taken into account in shaping decisions about European security.[46]

Even to the most ardently pro-Western, pro-democracy factions in Russia, the U.S. determination to consider any of the Soviet Union's former satellite nations for NATO membership should have been painfully evident. Conversely, Russia had no chance of receiving an invitation in the foreseeable future. The assertion that NATO was not directed against any country may have been a convenient fiction for U.S. leaders, but it was a fiction. Deterring and containing Russia was not the only purpose of NATO expansion; many U.S. and Western European officials genuinely wanted to spread and protect the blessings of democracy and free markets. But the lack of trust toward Russia—and the underlying goal of containing Moscow's power—also was apparent.

Yet even some realist scholars do not dismiss as brazen hypocrisy the statements of benign intent on the part of NATO expansion advocates. Mearsheimer, for example, contends that the strategy was not based on realist calculations that Russia was a threat that had to be deterred.

Instead, it was based "mainly on liberal principles, and its chief architects did not think Moscow should have seen it as threatening."[47] He also stresses that "the liberals within the Clinton administration had won the battle for NATO expansion" by the late 1990s and had "little difficulty" convincing like-minded types in Europe to endorse the project. In fact, "Western European elites may have been even more wedded than the Americans to the notion that an all-inclusive liberal order could maintain long-term peace in Europe."[48]

But it is not easy to separate that desire from the potent fear of Russia that dominated the views of the populations and officials throughout newly liberated Eastern Europe. In his memoirs, President Clinton mentions that such comments repeatedly punctuated his meetings with East European leaders.[49] He notes that Polish president Lech Wałęsa was especially apprehensive. "He was deeply suspicious of Russia and wanted Poland in NATO as soon as possible."[50] Given the history of Moscow's heavy-handed interactions with its smaller East European neighbors (during both the Soviet and czarist eras) such wariness about Russia was entirely understandable. Nevertheless, it was a mistake for American officials to let such concerns unduly influence U.S. policy regarding NATO expansion.

Mearsheimer concludes that liberal internationalist ideologues "came to dominate the discourse about European security so thoroughly during the first decade of the twenty-first century that further NATO expansion faced little opposition" from any source.[51] That was undoubtedly true in the United States. The first round of enlargement generated a fairly robust debate in the Senate and throughout the media and foreign policy communities. Nineteen senators voted against the measure in May 1998. Just five years later, the vote approving the second, more provocative, round was unanimous. Subsequent Senate votes on new NATO members have been unanimous or nearly so. In 2017, the chamber endorsed the admission of tiny Montenegro 97–2, with only Rand Paul (R-KY) and Mike Lee (R-UT) dissenting.[52]

A pervasive confidence in the efficacy of broadening NATO and other liberal Western institutions still seemed to animate U.S. and some European officials during the attempt to integrate Ukraine into those institutions over Moscow's vehement objections. Western leaders certainly have invoked the "liberal peace and reform" rationale publicly, and sometimes privately, throughout the expansion process.[53] In his memoirs, George W. Bush reflects that attitude when he expresses great personal pride in casting the U.S. vote at the alliance's November 2002 summit in Bucharest to extend membership invitations to four former Warsaw Pact countries and the three Baltic republics. His language is quite revealing. "I viewed NATO expansion as a powerful tool to advance the freedom agenda. Because NATO requires nations to meet high standards for economic and political openness, the possibility of membership acts as an incentive for reform."

Some U.S. leaders persisted in the official stance that NATO had no hostile intent toward Russia long after the credibility of that assurance was threadbare. In the midst of the 2014 Ukraine crisis, President Obama told an audience in Estonia that "our NATO Alliance is not aimed 'against' any other country."[54] But even in the unlikely event that U.S. policymakers throughout the post–Cold War period believed their own rhetoric about NATO's goals being benevolent and largely nonmilitary, that position was irrational. Secretary of Defense Robert Gates spoke a blunt truth at the February 2007 Munich Security Conference. Although his main focus was on getting greater burden sharing from the European allies, his remarks had a broader implication. "NATO is not a 'paper membership' or a 'social club' or a 'talk shop.' It is a *military* alliance—one with serious real-world obligations," he stressed.[55] Despite soothing words to the contrary from other Western officials, that also is how Russian leaders viewed the NATO that was steadily advancing toward their country's western border.

An excessive belief in the benefits of expanding liberal institutions, including NATO, may have driven some proponents of NATO expansion, but U.S. actions suggested the presence of other motives as well. As discussed in Chapter 3, some portions of the American foreign policy community never fully accepted or trusted Moscow, even when the Cold War ended and a democratic Russia emerged from the wreckage. And some wanted to flex America's power now that Washington's only serious geopolitical rival had collapsed and what Charles Krauthammer memorably described as the "unipolar moment"[56] had arrived. The unexpected power vacuum created an irresistible opportunity to consolidate America's status as a global hegemon, and some policymakers were determined to take advantage of the unipolar moment before it faded. NATO expansion was a key method of expanding and deepening U.S. hegemony in Europe.[57]

Texas A&M University professor Christopher Layne, author of *Peace of Illusions: American Grand Strategy from 1940 to the Present*, contends that after the end of the Cold War, NATO expansion took the form of "double enlargement." Not only did Washington push to expand NATO's membership, but U.S. officials were determined to expand the scope and nature of the alliance's mission. In the post–Cold War era, "America's, and NATO's, strategic concerns extended to Europe's peripheries," including the Baltic republics, Ukraine, North Africa, the Caucasus, and the Balkans.[58]

NATO's military meddling in the ethnic civil wars in Bosnia and Kosovo in the mid- and late 1990s lend support to Layne's argument that America's conception of strategic interests had expanded markedly—and that U.S. leaders believed NATO was the appropriate vehicle for advancing those broader interests and objectives. Even without the risk of a Soviet military move to block such a Western intervention, it is difficult to imagine that during the Cold War, NATO would have considered parochial squabbles in the Balkans important enough to warrant alliance combat missions.

The West's activist policy regarding developments in Georgia and Ukraine also confirm Layne's thesis about the dramatically expanded concept of U.S. interests, especially security interests. When they were constituent parts of the Soviet Union, those political entities obviously were not a concern to either the United States or NATO. Yet merely because they gained independence from Moscow's control when the USSR dissolved, those same entities supposedly became crucial to America's well-being. Indeed, they are so important that the United States and the other NATO members should be willing to incur grave risks to protect them from Russia. The strategic logic underlying such a fundamental policy shift, however, is hazy.

Expansion for the Sake of Expansion

The extent of NATO's membership growth has reached absurd proportions. When the United States insists on acquiring microstates such as Montenegro and Macedonia as allies, it is apparent that U.S. leaders have abandoned serious strategic rationales—or even rational strategic thought. Such allies are utterly dependent client states that bring no meaningful strategic assets to the table. The notion that they somehow advance NATO's or America's security is transparently laughable.

Daniel Larison, senior editor at the *American Conservative* magazine, concludes that "like nearby Montenegro, Macedonia is being offered alliance membership as a reward for political decisions that have nothing to do with enhancing the security of Europe and the United States." He adds that neither the United States nor NATO "is made more secure by adding more small states in the Balkans." Unfortunately, though, "NATO expansion keeps stumbling ahead like the zombie policy that it is. In a few years, the U.S. will be handing out another security guarantee that it doesn't need to make, and this will happen without any serious debate in Washington."[59]

Robert W. Merry, former editor of *Congressional Quarterly,* the *National Interest*, and the *American Conservative*, poses a pertinent question about NATO's continuing waves of expansion that entail memberships for ever-smaller countries. "Is Montenegro, with 5,332 square miles and some 620,000 citizens," Merry asks sarcastically, "really a crucial element in Europe's desperate project to protect itself against Putin's Russia?"[60] He puts his finger on both elements of the faulty reasoning of NATO enthusiasts. The Russian threat is greatly exaggerated, and new alliance members like Montenegro would be useless if a serious Russian threat did exist. NATO expansion is now a doubly bankrupt policy.

Yet NATO partisans typically act as though opposition to even this form of expansion is illegitimate. Indeed, they view criticism of making small, weak countries alliance members (and U.S. security dependents) as an unacceptable stance that threatens America's leadership position in the world. The overreaction sometimes reaches absurd and ugly proportions. One example was Senator John McCain's vitriolic denunciation in 2017 of fellow Republican Sen. Rand Paul, who had insisted that the

Senate should conduct a meaningful debate on approving NATO membership for Montenegro.

McCain noted Paul's previous opposition, but instead of countering his arguments, the Arizona senator resorted to nasty innuendos. If one opposed the measure promoting Montenegro's membership, he argued, "You are achieving the objectives of Vladimir Putin . . . trying to dismember this small country which has already been the subject of an attempted coup." McCain continued, "If they object, they are now carrying out the desires and ambitions of Vladimir Putin, and I do not say that lightly." He asked for unanimous consent for an immediate voice vote to rush the measure through. Paul invoked his senatorial privilege to object and insist on a floor debate and a roll call vote. McCain's infamous temper then erupted. "The only conclusion you can draw," he thundered, "is he has no justification for his objection to having a small nation be part of NATO that is under assault from the Russians. So, I repeat again, the senator from Kentucky is now working for Vladimir Putin."[61]

Larison justifiably rebukes McCain for his ad hominem attack on Paul. He also identifies a broader, unsavory motive for resorting to such tactics: "McCain's accusation is obnoxious, but it also shows how weak the case for bringing Montenegro into NATO is. If there were a strong argument in favor of adding a new member, McCain wouldn't have to stoop to attacking Paul as a Russian pawn, but there isn't and even he knows that."[62] The same could be said of other NATO partisans who reflexively embrace membership expansion for the sake of expansion and resent anyone who points out the lack of strategic logic.

Some alliance enthusiasts act as though prospective members have a moral and political obligation to join NATO if membership is on the table. That attitude was apparent in the aftermath of Macedonia's vote in the autumn of 2018.[63] Voters were asked to approve a crucial agreement to resolve Skopje's long-standing controversy with Greece over the name of the country by adopting the formal name Republic of North Macedonia.[64] That change would end Athens' objections to Skopje joining the EU or NATO and pave the way for membership in both bodies.

Voters did indeed endorse the agreement by a wide margin, with some 90 percent voting in favor. However, another requirement was that at least 50 percent of eligible voters had to cast ballots, and in a hugely disappointing turnout, only 37 percent did so. The reaction in the United States and other major NATO powers was troubling. Because the vote was advisory rather than binding, the U.S. State Department implicitly urged the Macedonian parliament to disregard the 50 percent requirement. The State Department released a statement declaring that Skopje should "take its rightful place in NATO and the EU" and that members of Macedonia's parliament ought to "rise above partisan politics and seize this historic opportunity."[65] The last point was crucial, because opposition parties controlled enough seats to make a two-thirds vote for approving the agreement and advancing Macedonia's NATO prospects problematic. Washington's apparent stance was that embracing the EU and NATO was the only acceptable option for the Macedonian people.

Intra-Alliance Spats Regarding Expansion

There is little evidence of meaningful disagreement among NATO members regarding a new round of expansion into the Balkans by admitting Montenegro and Macedonia, and possibly other small countries. Despite the disorders in the 1990s, the major NATO powers now seem to regard the region as a reasonably quiescent geostrategic backwater. As discussed in Chapter 4, that impression may not be entirely accurate, but neither the United States nor its principal European allies seem worried or exhibit disagreement about adding more Balkan ministates to the alliance.

The same bland consensus does not exist with regard to two other remaining candidates for admission, Georgia and Ukraine. Worries about those nations' proximity to Russia and Moscow's likely hostile reaction have induced greater caution in several NATO capitals. The lack of consensus is apparent and may be growing. Even as U.S. officials have continued to press for membership invitations to both countries, European NATO members remain split on the issue.

Some countries, especially in Eastern Europe, appear to embrace Washington's position, believing that the alliance must develop a stronger front against possible Russian aggression. East European countries that are most exposed to Russian power and most worried about the

Kremlin's goals are particularly supportive of additional NATO expansion, with respect to both the Balkans and Russia's immediate neighbors, Ukraine and Georgia.

Slovakia's foreign minister, Miroslav Lajčák, speaking at a security conference in Budapest on February 25, 2016, said it was obvious before the membership invitation was issued to Montenegro that NATO was divided about whether to continue the enlargement process. His own position was extremely clear. Referring to Russian involvement in the simmering conflict in eastern Ukraine, he emphasized that "rather than freezing NATO enlargement we think the trouble in Ukraine has only strengthened the case for it."[66]

Poland's minister of foreign affairs, Witold Waszczykowski, delivered an address to the parliament on February 9, 2017: "This year we will welcome Montenegro to the Alliance as a fully-fledged member. It shows that NATO is adhering to its open-door policy towards countries that are guided by a similar understanding of European security and that share the same values. We hope that this will not be the last stage of NATO's enlargement."[67] He explicitly cited Ukraine as one of the alliance's key strategic partners.

The pro-enlargement sentiment is most emphatic in the Baltic republics. On August 7, 2018, Latvia's ministry of foreign affairs released a statement marking the 10-year anniversary of the war between Russia and Georgia. It included the following:

> Latvia regards Georgia as an important partner to the North Atlantic Treaty Organisation (NATO), and being high on NATO's agenda. Latvia's position concerning Georgia's path to NATO remains unchanged. At the Bucharest Summit in 2008, it was agreed that Georgia would once (sic) become a member of the Alliance. That decision was also reaffirmed at the Brussels Summit in 2018. Doors to NATO are open, and third countries have no right of veto on the Alliance's decisions, which is confirmed by an invitation for Macedonia to begin accession talks to join NATO.[68]

Latvian Foreign Minister Edgars Rinkēvičs followed up the foreign ministry's statement with an even more emphatic and explicit endorsement of NATO membership for Georgia and Ukraine. He warned,

"What happened in Georgia in 2008, and then in Ukraine, convinces us that we have to do everything to prevent this from happening again." Rinkēvičs then emphasized that Latvia, Lithuania, and Poland wanted Georgia and Ukraine to become NATO members.[69]

Portions of "old Europe" still are decidedly less enthusiastic about welcoming Georgia and Ukraine into the alliance. France has remained strikingly adamant in its opposition. French president François Hollande candidly told a press conference in Paris on February 5, 2015, that Ukraine's NATO membership would be "undesirable" for France. "We must state it clearly, we should tell other countries the truth, including about what we are not ready to accept."[70] Hollande reiterated those sentiments at the NATO summit in Warsaw, Poland, the following year: "NATO has no role at all to be saying what Europe's relations with Russia should be. For France, Russia is not an adversary, not a threat."[71] The views of Hollande's successor, Emmanuel Macron, do not seem significantly different regarding the membership issue.

Some French lawmakers are equally convinced that adding Georgia or Ukraine to NATO is not in France's best interest. Aymeri de Montesquiou, a member of the French Senate, said at a meeting with the chairman of the Russian Duma, Sergey Naryshkin, in December 2015, "France and Germany are both categorically against Ukraine, Georgia and Moldova joining NATO." Both countries recognize that admitting any of those countries "would be an absolute provocation."[72]

Although opposition to membership for Georgia and Ukraine is less intense in other West European countries, wariness is evident. German Foreign Minister Frank-Walter Steinmeier was scarcely more receptive than Hollande to making Ukraine a NATO member, stating, "I see a partner relationship between Ukraine and NATO, but not membership."[73]

Wolfgang Ischinger, chairman of the Munich Security Conference and member of the Yalta European Strategy Conference Board, concluded in September 2017, "I cannot see any possibility on the horizon for all NATO members to vote in favor of Ukraine's membership. There is no chance of this happening while there is gunfire in [Ukraine]. The key problem is the conflict, which will prompt many NATO members to say: if we accept Ukraine, we inherit these problems with Russia."[74]

The Perils of Enlargement

As Robert Gates astutely pointed out, NATO is not a "social club." It is a military alliance with real-world, and potentially very dangerous, obligations. Too many advocates of bringing virtually every European country (except Russia, of course) into the alliance implicitly ignore that reality. And as long as nothing goes wrong, they can persist in their delusion that NATO is something other than a military alliance wielding enormously destructive weapons and that membership expansion is a benign, inoffensive act.

But the real world has a nasty habit of intruding on fantasies, and the NATO fantasy could turn very ugly indeed. In their much-noticed television interview, Tucker Carlson and President Trump dared to confront a genuine issue: Does it make sense for Americans to risk their lives and the lives of their loved ones to defend Montenegro?[75] A similar question could, and should, be asked about Slovakia, Estonia, and other nations on the growing roster of Washington's security dependents in NATO. Moreover, intelligent Americans need to ask themselves that question now, not in the midst of a crisis with possible thermonuclear implications.

Defenders of NATO expansion typically emphasize the legal aspect—asserting that Central and East European nations had every right under international law to decide if they wanted to join NATO and that Russia had no right to veto their choices. But that argument misses (or chooses to ignore) a fundamental point: legal considerations notwithstanding, the course that the United States and its allies adopted has had profound, negative geopolitical consequences.

Dimitri K. Simes, president of the Center for the National Interest, makes that important distinction even with respect to the first stage of NATO enlargement, noting that "the Clinton administration had every legal right to proceed with NATO expansion. What U.S. officials had no right to do was think that they could move NATO's borders further and further east without changing Russia's perception of the West from friend to adversary."[76] The course that U.S. and European leaders adopted has achieved exactly that unfortunate outcome.

CHAPTER 3

COMPARING THE SOVIET AND RUSSIAN "THREATS"

A crucial argument for not only preserving NATO but continuing to add new members and expand the alliance eastward is the dire security threat that Russia supposedly poses to Europe's democracies. The notion that Russia is a malicious and dangerous aggressor, much less one with no sense of limits, is at best a distortion and at worst a complete fallacy. Nevertheless, it is a pervasive belief in U.S. political, policy, and media circles, and it has generated intense resistance to any constructive change in Washington's policies regarding Russia or NATO. It also has been accompanied by the systematic smearing of Americans who dare criticize the conventional wisdom on either issue.[1] Even worse, exaggerating Russia's capabilities and aggressive tendencies has led to the adoption of hostile measures that have already plunged the United States into a second cold war.

U.S. policymakers and the American public both have an unfortunate tendency to conflate Russia with the Soviet Union—and conflate the challenges those two very different countries have posed to America's security and other interests. Senate Majority Leader Mitch McConnell expressed such a view explicitly in August 2018, saying "I think the Russians are acting like the old Soviet Union."[2] His comment was an especially direct manifestation of that simplistic attitude, but the more frequent, subtle versions are nearly as revealing—and corrosive.

Such anti-Russian sentiments have manifested in a variety of ways throughout the post–Cold War period.

In his memoirs, Donald Rumsfeld, George W. Bush's secretary of defense, could hardly contain his enthusiasm about NATO's continuing eastward expansion. Recalling his attendance at the June 2004 summit in Istanbul that welcomed seven former members of the Warsaw Pact to membership in NATO, Rumsfeld stated that he felt a "great sense of satisfaction" watching those countries join the Western alliance. "It was a vindication of the tough, nerve-wracking, long-sustained, costly, and high-minded half-century struggle by the allied countries, with bipartisan U.S. leadership, to contain and eventually defeat Soviet communism."[3]

He implicitly saw NATO expansion as the West's ultimate victory over the Soviet Union. Never mind that the USSR already was nearly 13 years in its grave and that NATO was marching eastward toward a democratic Russia, not the West's former totalitarian adversary. There was little indication that he made any such distinction, and Rumsfeld's attitude typified that of U.S. officials, both at the time and subsequently.

Viewing Russia as the same menace as America's Cold War nemesis actually has deepened in recent years. Shrill anti-Russian sentiments—and a corresponding hostility toward anyone advocating a more conciliatory Western policy toward Moscow—received a major boost with the media and political reaction to the July 2018 Helsinki summit between President Trump and Russian president Vladimir Putin. Trump's critics accused him of appeasing Putin, much as British prime minister Neville Chamberlain appeased Adolf Hitler at the 1938 Munich Conference.[4] Some opponents, including former CIA Director John Brennan and House Democratic Minority Whip Steny Hoyer (D-MD), even accused the president of committing treason for not doing enough to defend American interests and being too accommodating to the Russian leader.[5] CNN host Fareed Zakaria surpassed that condemnation, contending that "treasonous" was "too weak a word."[6]

Angry critics regarded Trump's solicitous behavior at Helsinki as an unforgivable offense because Russia supposedly poses an existential threat to the United States. Hostile pundits and politicians charged that Moscow's apparent interference in the 2016 U.S. elections constituted an attack on America akin to Pearl Harbor and 9/11.[7] It was not a new line of argument. Numerous examples of hyperbole about the "Russia threat" can be found long before the Helsinki summit. When National Security Advisor Michael Flynn was pressured to resign in early 2017, *New York Times* columnist Thomas Friedman described Russia's meddling as "a 9/11 scale event. They attacked the core of our democracy. That was a Pearl Harbor scale event."[8]

At a March 2017 House Homeland Security Committee session, Rep. Bonnie Watson Coleman (D-NJ) accused Russia of engaging in outright warfare against the United States. "I think this attack that we've experienced is a form of war, a form of war on our fundamental democratic principles."[9] During House Intelligence Committee hearings that same month, several of Coleman's Democratic colleagues made similar alarmist statements. Rep. Jackie Speier (D-CA) insisted that Russia's activities were "an act of war." Washington Democratic congressman Denny Heck explicitly compared Russia's actions to the Japanese attack on Pearl Harbor and the 9/11 terrorist attacks.[10] Such rhetorical threat inflation was not confined to House members. Sen. Ben Cardin (D-MD), the ranking Democrat on the Senate Foreign Relations Committee, similarly described the election meddling as an "attack" and likened it to a "political Pearl Harbor."[11]

When Special Counsel Robert Mueller obtained a grand jury indictment against Russian propagandists operating a so-called online troll farm, the equation of such activities with an act of war became commonplace. Jerrold Nadler (D-NY), the ranking Democrat on the House Judiciary Committee, asserted flatly that the troll farm's activities were "the equivalent of Pearl Harbor."[12]

There are several problems with such strident rhetoric. First, the hypocrisy is a bit thick, because the United States has meddled shamelessly in the political affairs of dozens of countries, including democratic countries, for decades.[13] Indeed, U.S. operatives, some of whom had close ties with Bill Clinton's administration, played major roles in Russian president Boris Yeltsin's 1996 reelection campaign.[14]

Second, the vitriol directed against Americans who favor a more restrained, accommodating policy toward Russia has reached levels not seen since the McCarthy era of the 1950s—and that development is poisoning the foreign policy debate. John McCain's ugly smear of Rand Paul merely for opposing Montenegro's bid for NATO membership is discussed in Chapter 2, but McCain was hardly unique in resorting to such slimy tactics. Writing for *Medium*, Greg Olear later enthusiastically endorsed McCain's scurrilous accusation that Paul was doing Putin's bidding. In a wildly speculative article titled "Red Paul: The Senator from Kentucky Is Now Working for Vladimir Putin," Olear excoriated Paul for trying to ease U.S.-Russian tensions.[15] Unfortunately, the tactics of personal destruction continue to proliferate, and a growing roster of political figures, journalists, and scholars are victims of such neo-McCarthyism.[16]

Third, using the terminology and imagery of warfare reflects, at the least, indifference to the dangers entailed in waging a second cold war with Moscow. Such an approach is irresponsible. Exacerbating already-worrisome tensions with Russia, the one country with the nuclear firepower to destroy American civilization, is profoundly unwise, since a cold war could always turn hot. And to raise the risk level merely in response to mundane election meddling is reckless.

Finally, equating Moscow's conduct with the Pearl Harbor and 9/11 attacks is illogical and calls into question either the sincerity or judgment of those making the comparison. The *Intercept*'s Glenn Greenwald highlights the obvious fallacy with such comparisons:

> The only specific proposal one hears now when it comes to responding to Russian meddling is a call for "sanctions." But if one really believes that Russia's actions amount to Pearl Harbor or 9/11, then sanctions seem like a very lame—indeed, a woefully inadequate—response. To borrow their rhetoric, imagine if Roosevelt had confined his response to Pearl Harbor to sanctions on Japanese leaders, or if Bush had announced sanctions on Al Qaeda as his sole response to 9/11. If you really believe this rhetoric, then you must support retaliation beyond mere sanctions.[17]

According to advocates of an uncompromising anti-Russia policy, Trump's performance at Helsinki stood in shameful contrast to the behavior of previous presidents toward Soviet leaders. McCain summarized that view in a press release: "No prior president has ever abased himself more abjectly before a tyrant. Not only did President Trump fail to speak the truth about an adversary; but speaking for America to the world, our president failed to defend all that makes us who we are—a republic of free people dedicated to the cause of liberty at home and abroad."[18] Other critics contrasted Trump's behavior with that of Ronald Reagan's firm stance, highlighting the latter's "evil empire" speech and his later demand that Mikhail Gorbachev tear down the Berlin Wall as examples of how Trump should have acted.[19]

Russia Is Not the Soviet Union

One problem with citing such examples is that they apply to a different country: the Soviet Union. Too many Americans act as though there is no meaningful difference between that entity and Russia. Worse still, U.S. leaders have embraced the same kind of uncompromising policies that Washington pursued to contain Soviet power.[20] It is a major blunder that has inexorably damaged relations with Moscow since the demise of the USSR at the end of 1991.

One obvious difference between the Soviet Union and Russia is that the Soviet governing elite embraced Marxism-Leninism and its objective of world revolution. Sometimes that professed allegiance was primarily a cover for Soviet imperialism, but in other instances, the fervor seemed genuine. In any case, the Kremlin allied with, sponsored, and assisted left-wing revolutionary movements around the world. Not only did it seek to undermine democratic and other anti-communist governments in Western Europe, Latin America, and other regions, the Soviet government became the political patron, financier, and arms supplier for communist or pro-communist regimes in places as diverse as Cuba, Nicaragua, North Vietnam, North Yemen, Afghanistan, and Angola. Washington had reason to be concerned about the extent not only of the USSR's totalitarian behavior at home, but of its international geopolitical agenda.

Today's Russia, though, is not a messianic revolutionary power. Columbia University professor Richard K. Betts makes the appropriate distinction succinctly: "Vladimir Putin's Russia is authoritarian, but unlike the Soviet Union, it is not the vanguard of a globe-spanning revolutionary ideal."[21] The differences are ideological, political, economic, and strategic.

Russia's economic system is a rather mundane form of corrupt crony capitalism, not rigid state socialism. The political system is a conservative autocracy with aspects of a rigged democracy, not a one-party dictatorship that brooks no dissent whatsoever. There is nothing akin to the terror that Joseph Stalin visited on millions of people whom his security apparatus merely suspected might harbor subversive sentiments. Putin's Russia does not maintain a vast network of prisons devoted to incarcerating political prisoners as Stalin and his successors did throughout the decades of communist rule.

Russia is hardly a Western-style democracy, but neither is it a continuation of the Soviet Union's horrifically brutal totalitarianism. Indeed, the country's political and social philosophy is quite different from that of its predecessor. For example, the Orthodox Church had no meaningful influence during the Soviet era—something that was unsurprising, given communism's official adherence to atheism. Soviet authorities strongly discouraged religious beliefs and activities with policies that involved systematic harassment and discrimination. A young Soviet citizen who wished to embark on a high-status career and progress through the bureaucratic ranks could not display the slightest religious inclination, or promotions would come to an abrupt halt. Indeed, even the most circumspect believer was wise to conceal such political heresy.

Frequently, the state's response went well beyond harassment and discrimination to outright persecution. A large percentage of inmates in the notorious gulags were religious dissidents. Indeed, communist officials tended to equate religious dissent with political dissent, and they showed no inclination to tolerate either version. That repression did not eradicate religious beliefs, but it did weaken them and drive them underground.

The situation is markedly different today. The church has a significant influence in Putin's Russia, especially on social issues. Gregory Freeze, the Victor and Gwendolyn Beinfield Professor of History at

Brandeis University and an expert on Russian social history, notes that "the patriarch and the president appear to be on very good terms."[22] Putin himself has urged Russians to return to more traditional and Christian values as embodied in the Orthodox Church. His blend of religious nationalism was evident in a 2013 speech in which he warned his fellow citizens to "avoid the example of European countries that were 'going away from their roots,' by legalising gay marriage" and approving other forms of social liberalism.[23] A Soviet leader also might have condemned such liberalism, but he would never have done so within the context of endorsing religious traditionalism.

To be sure, the church's revived influence is not necessarily good for individual rights. Although the clergy is not monolithic on social and political issues, Orthodox leaders exhibit a reactionary inclination. Their position on gay rights and their views about expressions of sexuality in movies, books, and online sites are rigid and intolerant. The church's perspective on immigrants is equally unenlightened. Overall, the church has promoted a dour culture in Russia on an array of issues. Many Orthodox clergy members are advocates of Russian chauvinism and embrace a policy of hostility to foreigners, thereby reinforcing the Putin government's nationalist inclinations.

The bottom line, though, is that Russia is a conventional, somewhat conservative power, whereas the Soviet Union was a totalitarian power that at least professed to be globalist and revolutionary. That's a rather large and meaningful difference, and U.S. policy needs to grasp that point. Unfortunately, some adamant critics of Russia try to spin the resurgence of political and social conservatism as a threat to the entire democratic West. Both former vice president Joe Biden and Michael McFaul, who served as ambassador to Moscow during Barack Obama's administration, epitomize that mentality.

Biden asserts that "the Russian government is brazenly assaulting the foundations of Western democracy around the world." According to Biden, Russia's moves against Georgia and Ukraine were designed not only "to block their integration into NATO or the EU," but to "send a message to other governments in the region that pursuing Western-backed democratic reforms will bring dire consequences." He adds that "more frequently and insidiously," Russia "has sought to weaken and subvert Western democracies from the inside by weaponizing information, cyberspace, energy, and corruption."[24] Such a distorted analysis borders on paranoia, and at the very least constitutes a grotesque oversimplification. There is very little evidence that Russia took action against Georgia and Ukraine because the Putin government was terrified of democratic reforms in those countries. Instead, Russian leaders worried that the United States aimed to make both countries military outposts and geostrategic pawns against Russia.[25]

McFaul goes even further than Biden in expressing alarm about Moscow's policy. He argues not only that the Kremlin is a unilateral force determined to undermine Western democracy, but that "Putin has anointed himself the leader of a renewed nationalist, conservative movement fighting a decadent West. To spread these ideas, the Russian government has made huge investments in television and radio stations, social media networks, and Internet 'troll farms,' and it has spent lavishly in support of like-minded politicians abroad."[26]

Despite the efforts of McFaul, Biden, and other Russophobes to conjure the image of Russia as the leader of a new "Authoritarian Nationalist International," the reality is far less impressive or threatening. Yes, Putin has cultivated closer relations with other conservative, autocratic powers, including China, Saudi Arabia, and Turkey, and he has refurbished Russia's relations with leftist autocracies, such as Cuba and Venezuela. Putin also has developed ties with right-wing populist political factions in Europe. However, he also has sought to improve relations with Japan, South Korea, Brazil, Mexico, and other countries with centrist democratic governments.[27]

The common denominator in Putin's policy appears to be a focus on pursuing initiatives with any partners that have the potential to advance Russia's national economic and security interests. That is little more than the routine diplomacy that even midlevel conventional powers have practiced throughout history. Given how the United States and most of its European allies have spurned and penalized Russia, no one should be surprised that the Kremlin has looked elsewhere for opportunities to establish political and economic partnerships. But such a pursuit of national interests falls far short of McFaul's thesis about Russia directing a new, subversive international movement.

The bottom line is that the Soviet Union was a global power (and, for a time, arguably a superpower) with global ambitions and capabilities to match. It not only controlled an empire in Eastern Europe, it cultivated and extensively assisted military allies and clients around the world, including in such far-flung places as Cuba, Vietnam, and Angola. The USSR also intensely contested the United States for influence in all of those arenas. Conversely, Russia is a regional power with limited extraregional reach. The Kremlin's ambitions focus heavily on the "near abroad," aimed at trying to block the eastward creep of NATO and the U.S.-led intrusion into Russia's core security zone. Not only are Russia's ambitions and capabilities decidedly more limited than those of its predecessor, Moscow's strategic orientation seems more defensive than offensive.

Do Russia's Actions in Ukraine Herald Rogue Expansionist Ambitions?

Those who contend that Russia's annexation of Crimea in 2014 proves that the Putin government is pursuing an aggressive, expansionist foreign policy are misreading the situation. Crimea was a special case for several reasons. First, the peninsula had been part of Russia between 1783 and 1954, during both the czarist and Soviet eras. Soviet leader Nikita Khrushchev, for reasons that are not entirely clear, arbitrarily transferred Crimea to Ukraine in 1954. Since Ukraine and Russia were both part of the Soviet Union, that decision didn't seem to matter much at the time. When the Soviet Union dissolved at the end of 1991, however, Russia suddenly faced the reality that its key naval base at Sevastopol now was on the territory of a foreign country. Yet even that development didn't seem to alarm Russian officials, since Ukraine's government remained in the hands of generally pro-Russian political leaders throughout the 1990s and the early years of the new millennium. Kiev provided further reassurance by granting Russia a 25-year lease on the facility shortly after gaining independence.

The situation became problematic, though, when Viktor Yushchenko, an anti-Russian, pro-Western figure, became Ukraine's president in 2004, leading the so-called Orange Revolution. Russian officials were noticeably nervous when Yushchenko indicated a renewal was unlikely when Moscow's lease at Sevastopol expired in 2017. That danger passed, however, once another pro-Russian politician, Viktor Yanukovych, won Ukraine's 2010 presidential election. Moscow's anxiety then receded.

Those worries resurfaced with a vengeance in 2014, though, when anti-Yanukovych demonstrators, encouraged if not actively aided by Washington and the European Union, overthrew the Ukrainian president nearly two years before his term expired.[28] Extremely nationalist, anti-Russian factions dominated the regime that emerged from the Maidan Revolution. Not only did the Crimean naval base now seem in jeopardy, but the new leaders avidly sought NATO membership for Ukraine—something that Washington had pushed for years.

The Kremlin responded quickly and decisively to the Ukraine developments. Barely disguised Russian special forces reinforced the normal garrison at Sevastopol and set up positions elsewhere on the peninsula. Pro-Russian political figures in Crimea immediately called for a referendum on secession from Ukraine, which was held days later and produced a predictably affirmative vote. Newly elected Crimean officials then asked that their territory be allowed to join the Russian Federation—a "request" that Moscow quickly granted.

U.S. anger at such a transparent territorial grab was volcanic. The Obama administration denounced the move, and Washington imposed an array of economic sanctions on Russia. The administration also induced and pressured its European allies to do the same. Such a response constituted an overreaction, and a hypocritical one. Much of the blame for the Crimea episode should be put at Washington's door. The U.S.-EU meddling in Ukraine's politics to encourage the ouster of a pro-Russian government—a democratically elected one at that—could hardly be seen as other than hostile and threatening to both Russian leaders and the Russian public. Indeed, polls indicated that Putin's approval rating soared to over 80 percent following the annexation.[29]

The Crimea issue became the principal grievance that anti-Russia types in the United States cited to justify a confrontational policy—until the allegations of Russian interference in U.S. elections eclipsed that complaint. But one might ask why so many U.S. political leaders and policymakers elevated a parochial territorial dispute to such prominence, much less why they insist that the arbitrary edict made back in 1954 by the communist dictator of a defunct country must be treated with reverence.[30] It would have been better if the successor republics collectively had addressed and implemented territorial adjustments involving Crimea and other potential problem areas when the USSR dissolved, but Moscow's decision to resolve the Crimea question unilaterally was not necessarily a sign of broader territorial ambitions.

The conquest is not even unprecedented in the post–World War II era. Israel seized the Golan Heights from Syria in 1967 during the Six-Day War and later annexed that territory. Turkey seized a major portion of Cyprus and continues to occupy that land, establishing a puppet state as a façade. It is certainly an overstatement to contend, as does UCLA political science professor Daniel Treisman, that "By annexing a neighboring country's territory by force, Putin overturned in a single stroke the assumption on which the post–Cold War European order had rested."[31] One could make a stronger case that the first major blow to that post–Cold War European order came 15 years earlier when the Western powers amputated Kosovo from Serbia.

Yet Western opinion leaders routinely cite the Crimea annexation and Moscow's subsequent assistance to secessionist factions in eastern Ukraine as proof that Russia has broad, perhaps even unlimited, expansionist goals. In February 2015, Gen. Sir Adrian Bradshaw, the senior British officer in NATO, asserted that Russia's expansionism threatened to become an "obvious existential threat to our whole being."[32] The following year, Leon Panetta, the former secretary of defense, expressed similar alarm. "Let's not kid anybody," Panetta stated, "Putin's main interest is to try to restore the old Soviet Union."[33]

When advocates of a confrontational policy toward Moscow were not alleging that Putin wanted to revive the Soviet Union, they accused him of seeking to restore the pre-Soviet Russian empire. That allegation even predated the seizure of Crimea. Senator McCain made the accusation in 2008, at the time of the Russo-Georgian war. "I think it's very clear that Russian ambitions are to restore the old Russian Empire," McCain stated. "Not the Soviet Union, but the Russian Empire."[34]

That line of argument at least implicitly acknowledged that Putin was not a doctrinaire communist, but it still was misplaced and exaggerated. As Harvard University professor Andrei Shleifer and his co-author Daniel Treisman observe in *Foreign Affairs*, "To many in the West, Russia's 2008 invasion of Georgia seemed to prove the Kremlin's land hunger." Shleifer and Treisman argue that such a conclusion reflects poor logic. "Kremlin leaders bent on expansion would surely have ordered troops all the way to Tbilisi to depose [Georgia President Mikheil] Saakashvili. At the least, Russian forces would have taken control of the oil and gas pipelines that cross Georgia." Instead, the Russians "left those pipelines alone and quickly withdrew to the mountains."[35]

Shleifer and Treisman raise a very important point. If Putin is a rogue leader with massive expansionist objectives, why would he relinquish territory that Russian forces already occupied? Indeed, with very little additional effort, those forces could have captured Tbilisi and the rest of Georgia. Yet Moscow did not attempt to do so. Hitler never willingly gave up any of his conquests. And until the East European satellite empire collapsed in 1989–1991, the USSR disgorged only one occupied area—the portion of Austria it controlled at the end of World War II. Even that modest retreat took place only after laborious, multiyear negotiations for a treaty guaranteeing Austria's strict neutrality. If Putin truly harbors malignant expansionist ambitions comparable to those of Hitler and Stalin, declining to conquer and absorb all of Georgia when that achievement was easily within reach is a curious step. His decision merely to maintain and consolidate Abkhazia and South Ossetia as Russian protectorates suggests much more restrained and limited ambitions.

Allegations that Putin wants to reconstitute the Soviet or the czarist empires are vastly overblown. Former NATO supreme commander Gen. Philip M. Breedlove is a little closer to the mark when he contends that "Moscow is determined to reestablish what it considers its rightful sphere of influence, undermine NATO, and reclaim its great power status."[36] But wanting, indeed insisting upon, a sphere of influence has long been standard behavior for major powers. Indeed, the United States declared such a sphere when James Monroe's administration proclaimed the Monroe Doctrine—and it did so at a time when the country was still far from attaining great power status. As for wishing to undermine NATO, it is more accurate to say that Moscow is belatedly trying to fend off the alliance's seemingly inexorable advance east. Finally, Russian leaders would presumably like to reclaim great power status for their country; at the very least, they insist on a seat at the table when major decisions about Eastern Europe, the Middle East, and Central Asia are made. That position is not unreasonable, and an especially clumsy aspect of Western policy toward Moscow has been the unwillingness to accord even basic respect to Russia and not trample on its core interests.

Deception and displays of contempt toward Moscow have characterized the conduct of the United States and its NATO allies even outside the European arena. A prime example was their actions with respect to the military intervention in Libya. Western officials went to great lengths to reassure Russia (and China) that the proposed mission against Muammar Qaddafi was purely a humanitarian venture to prevent the slaughter of innocent civilians. Both of those powers worried that NATO might have regime-change ambitions that would set another undesirable precedent, reinforcing the Kosovo and Iraq precedents. Both Moscow and Beijing were surprisingly trusting, abstaining when the United Nations Security Council passed a resolution not only imposing a no-fly zone, but authorizing members to use "all necessary measures" and "appropriate means" to protect "civilians and civilian population centers under threat." Such vague language created a gigantic loophole.

The language of the resolution was crucial. Indeed, the emphasis on protecting civilians was the reason that Russia and China withheld their vetoes. The "protect civilians" provision soon proved to be nothing more than a cynical cover, however. Almost immediately, U.S. and other NATO planes, as well as cruise missiles, began to attack Qaddafi's air defenses and other targets that posed no threat to civilians but had everything to do with which side would win the civil war. Yet U.S. leaders from President Obama on down still parroted the official humanitarian rationale, even when it became obvious that the goal was far broader.[37] In her memoirs, Secretary of State Hillary Clinton still strongly denied that there had been any attempt to mislead Russia about the nature and purpose of the Libya intervention.[38]

Russian officials had a very different perspective, as Secretary of Defense Robert Gates recalled all too clearly:

> The Russians later firmly believed they had been deceived on Libya. They had been persuaded to abstain at the UN on the grounds that the resolution provided for a humanitarian mission to prevent the slaughter of civilians. Yet as the list of bombing targets steadily grew, it became obvious that very few targets were off-limits, and that NATO was intent on getting rid of Qaddafi. Convinced they had been tricked, the Russians would subsequently block any such future resolutions, including against President Bashar al-Assad in Syria.[39]

The Obama administration's response to Moscow's reluctance to be gulled again was the foreign policy equivalent of a temper tantrum.[40] Both Clinton and UN Ambassador Susan Rice excoriated the Russians for blocking action on Syria. On one occasion, Rice fumed that her country was "disgusted" by Russia and China's decision to veto a UN Security Council resolution condemning the violence in Syria and calling for an immediate end to that bloodshed. "The international community must protect the Syrian people from this abhorrent brutality," she asserted. "But a couple members of this council remain steadfast in their willingness to sell out the Syrian people and shield a craven tyrant." Their actions, she added, were "shameful" and "unforgivable."[41] Secretary Clinton termed them "despicable."[42]

At a minimum, Rice and Clinton needed a refresher course in diplomatic language. Moreover, after the West's deception regarding Libya—and Kosovo and NATO expansion—Washington's expectation that Moscow would blindly accept assurances about a supposedly limited humanitarian mission in Syria reflected supreme arrogance. With the Libya regime-change intervention, the United States and its NATO partners had destroyed what was left of Russian trust.

Russophobia and a New Cold War

Not surprisingly, warnings about the Kremlin's allegedly vast expansionist ambitions have proliferated in the years since the Crimea annexation. Ultrahawkish writer Ralph Peters asserted that Putin had a detailed plan to reclaim the Russian empire. "Make no mistake," Peters warned, "Putin truly believes he's entitled to reclaim Ukraine and a great deal more. In his view, independent capitals from Warsaw (yes, Warsaw) to Bishkek [Kyrgyz Republic's capital] are integral and natural parts of the Russian imperium. He regards them as property stolen from its rightful owner: Moscow."[43]

Eastern European officials have worked assiduously to fan such fears. In March 2017, Ukraine's foreign minister, Pavlo Klimkin, insisted that Moscow's expansionist targets went far beyond Ukraine. "Russia's appetite for hegemony does not stop with Ukraine," Klimkin warned. "It greedily eyes other former states and satellites of the Soviet Union, and more broadly seeks to destabilise and divide the rest of Europe and the wider transatlantic alliance."[44] Russia, he emphasized, posed a threat to the entire Western world and the liberal international order it maintains.

Shrill warnings about Russia's behavior resurfaced and intensified following the November 2018 clash between Ukrainian and Russian naval ships in the Kerch Strait (see Chapter 4). The usual Russophobes in the Western news media immediately speculated that the seizure of the Ukrainian ships might well be the opening move in another "land grab" against Ukraine similar to the takeover of Crimea.[45] Ukrainian president Petro Poroshenko insisted that Putin's goal was nothing less than to take over all of Ukraine.[46] Yet there was no tangible evidence of plans for even a limited, much less such a massive, impending territorial conquest of Ukraine.

In her address to the UN Security Council, U.S. Ambassador Nikki Haley blasted Moscow for "outlaw actions" and stated that the latest "outrageous violation of sovereign Ukrainian territory is part of a pattern of Russian behavior."[47] Former CIA station chief Daniel Hoffman asserted, "Containment and deterrence are vestiges of the Cold War, which effectively countered the Soviet Union. They are similarly applicable today because Putin—the KGB operative in the Kremlin reviving the ethos of the Soviet evil empire—would best be countered with a 21st-century version of President Reagan's 'peace through strength' strategy. Ukraine is on the front lines of defense against Russia's pernicious espionage, military, cyber and economic attacks. The time is ripe for U.S. leadership, and Ukraine's sovereignty is where we should draw and enforce a red line."[48]

One could scarcely imagine a more blatant and simplistic attempt to equate today's Russia with the totalitarian and messianic expansionist Soviet Union. Hoffman's proposal to "draw and enforce a red line" to protect Ukraine also would erase any meaningful distinction between Washington's security obligations to NATO members and European nonmembers. Kiev would have an Article 5 guarantee in all but name, and that would be an appallingly reckless, provocative step. A scholar for the staunchly pro-NATO Atlantic Council seemed to embrace reasoning similar to Hoffman's, speculating that although the alliance probably would not send combat units to defend Ukraine in response to further Russian encroachments, it might well dispatch "military advisers" to assist Kiev's forces.[49] The role of such American "advisers" in Vietnam, Syria, Yemen, and other arenas suggests just how perilous such a move might be.

The angry Western response to Russia's behavior in and around Crimea over the past five years is overdone.[50] Because of its size, geographic position, and both economic and strategic importance, Ukraine occupies a special position in Moscow's geopolitical calculations. Russian leaders are even more concerned about the prospect of Ukraine becoming a NATO outpost than they are about Georgia doing so. Other portions of the Soviet Union's former domain do not generate the same level of worry or determination. Yet despite the country's critical importance, there is little evidence that the Putin regime seeks to reabsorb Ukraine into a "Greater Russia." Russian leaders likely understand the difficulty of trying to rule directly a seething Ukraine—or even control it indirectly by installing a puppet government. The idea would soon evoke memories of the USSR's unhappy experiences in such places as Hungary, Czechoslovakia, and Afghanistan.

There is even less evidence that the Kremlin has ambitions to reincorporate the Baltic republics, Finland, or Poland, although they were also part of the czarist empire. Russian claims to Crimea were much stronger than claims to any of those states, and the strategic motivations were stronger too—especially after the Western-backed Maidan Revolution. The Russian government's actions regarding Crimea, even the annexation, seem more likely a defensive (over)reaction to a flagrant Western incursion into Russia's security space rather than the opening salvo in a vast expansionist campaign. Hillary Clinton and others who professed to see in Vladimir Putin's seizure of Crimea a repetition of Hitler's moves in the late 1930s make an unwarranted, over-the-top comparison.[51] That interpretation of events is also a false rationale for preserving, much less expanding, NATO.

As Klimkin's comments illustrate, NATO's East European members (as well as their fans in the United States) presumably are highlighting Russia's actions in Crimea to seek greater security assurances. Following the 2014 annexation, Estonian president Kersti Kaljulaid warned that "in 2008, they moved on Georgia. . . . I am afraid now that the resolve of the Western countries may not hold in the case of Ukraine. We need to stand very firm against giving again a message to Putin that it will blow over."[52] German chancellor Angela Merkel emphasized the deleterious impact of Moscow's actions in Ukraine, especially on the former Soviet satellite nations. She charged that Moscow had undermined European security in "words and deeds" by infringing on Ukraine's borders and "profoundly disturbed" NATO's eastern members who "therefore require the unambiguous back-up of the alliance."[53] Edgars Rinkēvičs, Latvia's minister of foreign affairs, was even more specific. "We have to be prepared that 'the little green men' [disguised Russian military personnel] may try to create confusion, just like they did in Crimea," he said.[54]

The barrage of apocalyptic warnings has continued and even grown. Most East European leaders, with the notable exception of Hungary's Victor Orbán, exhibit no trace of doubt that Russia is a dangerous, menacing power. In a March 2017 interview, Dalia Grybauskaitė, president of Lithuania, stated bluntly: "Russia is a threat not only to Lithuania but to the whole region and to all of Europe. We see how Russia is behaving in Kaliningrad, a Russian enclave on our border. There they have deployed nuclear-capable missiles that can reach European capitals.

It is not just about the Baltic region anymore."[55] Poland's foreign minister, Witold Waszczykowski, was equally alarmist, insisting that Russia's behavior posed an "existential threat" to Poland and the rest of democratic Europe even greater than ISIS.[56]

Despite the upsurge in such dire warnings, most of those same countries have not translated their professed alarm into drastic efforts to strengthen their own military capacities. Although some countries have increased military spending modestly, the actions the eastern European nations have undertaken do not come close to matching their apocalyptic warnings. Their principal response has been to demand that the United States do more to protect them from Russia.

The continuing mismatch between rhetoric and action raises obvious questions about how seriously they really take the alleged Russian threat. One would think that if the threat were truly existential, NATO's European members—especially those in the East—would be engaged in crash programs to strengthen their militaries. Yet signs of such determination are mild and limited, as discussed in Chapter 5.

The discrepancy suggests that policymakers in those countries have reached one of two conclusions. Either they don't really consider the Russian threat all that serious, despite their rhetoric to the contrary, or they are counting heavily on the United States to protect them. Either possibility—but especially the latter—should be unacceptable to the U.S. government and the American people. Believing that Americans should care about Europe's security is one thing. Believing that Americans should care more about Europe's security than the Europeans do is quite another. Washington's NATO partners need to fund more serious efforts to deter the alleged Russian threat, or they need to stop wailing about the dire nature of that threat.

Putting Relations with Russia into Perspective

Despite the shrill warnings of some NATO members and hawkish types in the United States, the great "Russia Threat" appears to be highly exaggerated. True, Russia is still a significant regional power militarily and economically, but it is not a global power or even a credible candidate to be a regional hegemon. The Kremlin would have difficulty executing anything more than a very limited expansionist agenda, even if it has one. Russia lacks the economic and military wherewithal for conducting a vast wave of aggression and territorial conquest.

The difference in economic and demographic features between the USSR and Russia is massive. The Soviet Union was the world's number two economic power, second only to the United States. Russia has an economy roughly the size of Canada's, and it is no longer ranked even in the global top 10.[57] Even taking into account purchasing power parity, Russia is still a second-tier economic player that is not in the same league as leading economic powers such as Japan, China, and Germany—much less the United States. It also has only three-quarters of the Soviet Union's territory (much of which consists of nearly empty Siberia) and barely half the population of the old USSR. If those limitations were not enough, it has a shrinking population afflicted with an assortment of public health problems, especially rampant alcoholism.[58] Today's Russia is merely a first-tier regional power with limited extraregional interests and reach. It is not by any stretch of the imagination a superpower.

All of these factors should make clear that Russia is not a credible global rival, much less an existential threat to the United States and its democratic system. Russia's power is a mere shadow of the Soviet Union's. True, Putin has sought to rebuild and modernize Russia's military, and has had some success in doing so.[59] Russia's navy once again includes some modern vessels, and the air force is now flying modern, and even some cutting-edge, aircraft. Putin's regime also has focused on developing and deploying long-range, precision-guided weapons and is pursuing considerable military research and development efforts, especially with respect to hypersonic aircraft and missiles.

Even those trends must be put into perspective, however. The restoration and modernization follow a decade of military decline and decay during the 1990s under Boris Yeltsin. Moreover, Moscow's 2018 military budget was a modest \$63.1 billion.[60] Not only was that amount dwarfed by the gargantuan U.S. military budget of \$643.3 billion, but it is also far less than China's \$168.2 billion and only slightly more than India's \$57.9 billion or France's \$53.4 billion.[61] Perhaps most significant, in contrast to the robust annual increases in U.S. spending levels, Russia's military spending is declining, not rising.[62] The 2017 budget was $69.2 billion, some $6.1 billion greater than the subsequent budget. That is an odd trend for a government that supposedly harbors vast offensive ambitions.

The only undiminished source of clout is Moscow's large nuclear arsenal. Of course, nuclear weapons are the ultimate deterrent. But they are not very useful for power projection or warfighting, except in the highly improbable event that a country's political leadership is eager to risk national and personal suicide.[63] And no evidence whatsoever suggests Putin and his oligarch backers are suicidal. Quite the contrary, they seem wedded to accumulating ever greater wealth and perks.

Finally, Russia's security interests actually overlap modestly with America's—most notably the desire to combat radical Islamic terrorism. If U.S. leaders did not insist on pursuing provocative, intrusive policies such as expanding NATO to Russia's border, undermining longtime Russian clients in the Balkans (Serbia) and the Middle East (Syria), and excluding Russia from key international economic institutions (such as the former Group of 8 [G-8], now G-7), there would be relatively few occasions when important American and Russian interests collide.

A fundamental shift in U.S. policy is needed, but that requires a major change in America's national psychology. For more than four decades, Americans saw (and were told to regard) the Soviet Union as a mortal threat to the nation's security and its most cherished values of freedom and democracy. Unfortunately, a mental reset did not take place when the USSR dissolved and a quasi-democratic Russia emerged as one of the successor states.

Too many Americans, including political leaders and policymakers, act as though we are still confronting the Soviet Union at the height of its power and ambitions. That obsolete view is causing multiple problems. Writing in 2016, Dimitri K. Simes, president of the Center for the National Interest, concluded that Western actions had produced an ominous situation. "Russia today is increasingly an angry, nationalistic, elective monarchy, and while it is still open for business with America and its allies, its leaders often assume the worst about Western intentions." As he noted, that unhappy situation was not inevitable. "Vladimir Putin's Russia is not a superpower, and its top officials are realistic about their country's military, geopolitical and economic limitations. Russia does not have a universal ideology predicated on the West as an enemy."[64]

Richard Betts likewise cautions that the West is overreacting to an (inflated) perception of a Russian threat. "Russia's intentions constitute no more of a threat than its capabilities," he concludes. "During the twentieth century, there were intense territorial conflicts between the two sides and a titanic struggle between them over whose ideology would dominate the world."[65] Those considerations no longer apply, but the United States and its NATO allies act as though little or nothing has changed.

It will be the ultimate tragic irony if, having avoided war with a messianic, totalitarian global adversary, we now stumble into war because of an out-of-date image of and policy toward a conventional, declining regional power. Yet unless U.S. leaders change both their mindsets and their policies toward Russia, especially their policy regarding NATO, that outcome is a very real possibility.

Washington's Longstanding Tone-Deaf Policy toward Russia

Ample signs of Moscow's growing irritation at being treated as an adversary by the United States and its NATO allies appeared long before the Ukraine crisis triggered a full-blown new cold war. Russian anger had been building for a long time. Boris Yeltsin's negative reaction to the first round of NATO expansion in the late 1990s was noted in Chapter 2, and other Russian officials expressed similar concerns and suspicions. Matters grew worse after the second round of expansion in 2004 and other moves that George W. Bush's administration adopted. The expansion process was indicative of a Western attitude that provoked and alarmed Russia. In a 2013 *Foreign Affairs* article, Betts observed that "to Moscow, it must seem that the Cold War is only half over, since the West's deterrence posture, although muted, lives on."[66] Since the Ukraine imbroglio erupted, the posture and the hostility it embodies isn't even all that muted.

One move that annoyed the Kremlin was Washington's plan to deploy a missile defense system based in Poland and the Czech Republic.

The United States formally proposed the system in 2007 but had been in talks with its new NATO allies about the idea since 2002. Bush asserted that the system was needed to protect Europe from a possible Iranian missile attack, and he flatly denied that it was aimed at Russia.[67] Critics pointed out that Tehran did not have missiles with that range, so the U.S scheme was, at the very least, premature. (Indeed, credible evidence of that capability didn't emerge until a December 2018 report indicating that Tehran finally may have developed such missiles.[68]) Moreover, locating the batteries in Central Europe to guard against a supposed threat from Iran seemed more than a little disingenuous to Putin and other Russian leaders. They suspected, quite logically, that the missile shield's real purpose was to intimidate Russia and degrade that country's offensive missile capability.[69]

Robert Gates, who served as secretary of defense during the final years of the Bush administration and the early years of the Obama administration, describes Putin's reaction to the missile defense plan and already existing examples of other U.S. policies directed at Russia. Speaking at the annual Munich Security Conference in February 2007, Putin "launched into a diatribe against the United States." The Russian president accused Washington of seeking a unipolar world dominated by the United States and that this approach was destabilizing the world. He lamented the "almost unconstrained hyper-use of force." Although that comment clearly referred to the decision to invade and occupy Iraq, Putin also had major concerns about U.S. policy in Europe. Gates recalls that "Putin asked why the United States was creating frontline bases with up to 5,000 troops on Russia's borders; why NATO was expanding aggressively toward a nonthreatening Russia; and why a missile defense system was being deployed on the Russian border."[70] Those were all very good questions that most American officials did not wish to address.

Gates is one of the few policymakers in the Clinton, Bush, or Obama administrations who took Russia's concerns seriously, and he concludes that Washington's handling of the bilateral relationship had been rather clumsy and insensitive from the beginning. "When I reported to the president my take on the Munich conference, I shared my belief that from 1993 onward, the West, and particularly the United States, had badly underestimated the magnitude of the Russian humiliation in losing the Cold War." Yet even that blunt assessment given to Bush did not fully capture Gates's views on the issue. "What I didn't tell the president was that I believed the relationship with Russia had been badly mismanaged after Bush left office in 1993. Getting Gorbachev to acquiesce to a unified Germany as a member of NATO had been a huge accomplishment. But moving so quickly after the collapse of the Soviet Union to incorporate so many of its formerly subjugated states into NATO was a mistake." Specific U.S. actions were ill-considered as well, in Gates's view. "U.S. agreements with the Romanian and Bulgarian governments to rotate troops through bases in those countries was a needless provocation."[71]

His list of foolish Western actions went on. "The Russians had long historical ties with Serbia, which we largely ignored." And in an implicit rebuke to his boss, Gates asserted that "trying to bring Georgia and Ukraine into NATO was truly overreaching." That move was a case of "recklessly ignoring what the Russians considered their own vital national interests."[72]

Gates's overall assessment of Western, especially U.S., policy toward Russia during the post–Cold War era was unsparingly harsh—and devastatingly accurate. "When Russia was weak in the 1990s and beyond, we did not take Russian interests seriously. We did a poor job of seeing the world from their point of view and managing the relationship for the long term."[73] Unfortunately, Gates is one of the rare anomalies in the American foreign policy community regarding policy toward Russia.

His criticism, trenchant as it is, still understates the folly of the policies that the United States and its NATO allies have pursued toward Moscow. The treatment that three successive U.S. administrations meted out to a newly capitalist, initially democratic Russia was appallingly myopic. Even before Vladimir Putin came to power—and long before Russia descended into illiberal democracy and then became an outright authoritarian state—the Western powers treated the country as a de facto enemy. The NATO nations engaged in a series of provocations even though Moscow had engaged in no aggressive conduct that could arguably have justified such actions.

Far too many Western (especially American) analyses explicitly or implicitly proceed as though the United States and its NATO allies worked to establish cordial relations with Russia but were compelled to adopt more hardline policies because of Russia's perversely aggressive conduct. That is a distorted, self-serving portrayal on the part of NATO partisans. It falsely portrays the West as purely a reactive player—implying that NATO initiatives were never insensitive, provocative, or aggressive. Nothing could be further from the truth. Indeed, the opposite is closer to the mark: Russia's actions, in terms of both timing and virulence, tended to be responses to Western provocations. Unfortunately, avid NATO supporters seem determined to double down, insisting that the Trump administration adopt even more uncompromising policies.[74]

Contending that Moscow is to blame for the deterioration of East-West relations because of its military actions in Georgia and Ukraine is especially inaccurate. The problems began much earlier than the events in 2008 and 2014. The West humiliated a defeated adversary that showed every sign of wanting to become part of a broader Western community. Expanding NATO and trampling on Russian interests in the Balkans were momentous early measures that torpedoed friendly relations. Such policy myopia was reminiscent of how the victorious allies inflicted harsh treatment on a defeated but newly democratic Weimar Germany after World War I.

Robert W. Merry, former editor of *Congressional Quarterly* and other prominent publications, provides a poignant analysis of the blundering U.S. policy toward Russia. "Rather than accepting as a great benefit the favorable developments enhancing Western security—the Soviet military retreat, the territorial reversal, the Soviet demise—the West turned NATO into a territorial aggressor of its own, absorbing nations that had been part of the Soviet sphere of control and pushing right up to the Russian border." Whereas Soviet troops in Central Europe during the Cold War were merely a few hundred miles from major Western capitals (constituting a menacing posture), now "Moscow is merely 200 miles from Western troops."

Merry adds, "Since the end of the Cold War, NATO has absorbed 13 nations, some on the Russian border, others bordering lands that had been part of Russia's sphere of influence for centuries. This constitutes a policy of encirclement, which no nation can accept without protest or pushback." Worse, "if NATO were to absorb those lands of traditional Russian influence—particularly Ukraine and Georgia—that would constitute a major threat to Russian security, as Russian president Vladimir Putin has sought to emphasize to Western leaders for years." Merry rightly concludes that the underlying problem "is the West's inability to perceive how changed geopolitical circumstances might require a changed geopolitical strategy."[75]

Such an inability is not merely frustrating, it is potentially disastrous. The NATO powers have treated Russia as an enemy, and there is now serious danger that it is becoming one.

CHAPTER 4

A SOBER RISK-BENEFIT CALCULATION FOR AMERICA

Far more important than the issue of burden sharing are the additional security obligations and risks that the United States has undertaken because of the decision to expand NATO eastward. As of late 2018, membership in the alliance had grown from 16 at the end of the Cold War to 29. The new members include a few fairly sizable and significant countries such as Poland, the Czech Republic, Hungary, and Romania, but most are small countries that add no measurable strategic capabilities to the alliance or to the United States. Indeed, calling such members U.S. "allies" is a misnomer; they are more accurately described as security dependents. Without exception, those countries bring more liabilities than assets to the table.

The addition of such tiny countries as the three Baltic republics (Estonia, Latvia, and Lithuania) epitomizes the process of indiscriminate NATO enlargement. The Baltic countries at least had credible economies, although little in the way of military capabilities. But NATO's willingness to admit members, no matter how small and weak, has become even worse. That point is striking with the more recent additions of Balkan ministates such as Montenegro and Macedonia. Montenegro's population is barely 629,000, and the country is best known for being the plot location of the James Bond movie *Casino Royale.* Even if one ignores Montenegro's disturbing reputation as a haven for organized crime in southeastern Europe, it fields a military of just 2,000 troops. Numerous American cities have larger populations, and their governments deploy more armed personnel; New York City alone has more than 34,000 uniformed police.

Regarding such a country as a worthwhile U.S. security ally borders on delusional. Cato Institute senior fellow Doug Bandow puts the matter well when he contends that NATO is now adding members with the same casual attitude that some people add Facebook friends.[1] There is one crucial difference, however. Facebook friends cannot involve anyone in a bloody armed conflict; fellow members of a military alliance can—and as history shows, they have done so frequently. The catastrophe of World War I is a prime example of how a small ally (Serbia) entangled its patron (czarist Russia) in a war that ultimately led not only to the demise of that great power, but also to the disintegration of several other European empires, combined with loss of life and destruction of property on an unprecedented scale.

A key drawback for the United States as it undertakes mushrooming security obligations in Eastern Europe is that any member of an alliance will have its own set of distinct national interests, and those interests sometimes lead to disputes, quarrels, and conflicts with neighboring states. In the case of NATO's expansion eastward, such tensions sometimes involve frosty relations between the new member and Russia, creating additional risks for the United States. Even when a possible confrontation with Russia is not the principal danger, taking on the obligation of defending a new alliance partner entails the risk of America becoming entangled in petty subregional spats that have little or no relevance to the republic's genuine national interests.

Security Dependents and Their Parochial Quarrels

A prime example of that problem is the baggage that comes with acquiring the tiny new allies in the Balkans. When Fox News host Tucker Carlson pointedly asked President Trump why he (Carlson) should send his son to die defending Montenegro, the president surprisingly seemed to repudiate his own administration's policy. His response indicated that Americans *shouldn't* be willing to sacrifice their lives for such a trivial ally. Furthermore, Trump warned that Montenegro "has very aggressive people. They may get aggressive, and congratulations, you're in World War III."[2]

As Bandow points out, Trump's comment was odd on two counts. First, the Senate approved the admission of Montenegro on Trump's watch in March 2017. If he thought that adding such a strategically useless and volatile ministate to the alliance was unwise, he could have withdrawn the treaty from consideration before the Senate vote. Second, as Bandow notes archly, while "it is theoretically possible that the vast, aggressive, powerful Montenegrin legions might launch themselves towards Moscow," it isn't too likely, because Montenegrin leaders "do not appear to have entirely lost their minds."[3]

Moscow does have longstanding military, economic, and political interests in the Balkans. And some evidence suggests the Kremlin may have interfered in Montenegro's domestic politics in an attempt to reverse the country's request to join NATO.[4] Nevertheless, the scenario in which a small Balkan NATO partner might trigger a major war with Russia is unlikely. A far more probable risk for America is that Montenegro or another alliance member could become embroiled in a parochial quarrel with one of its regional neighbors that escalates out of control and eventually entangles the United States. That scenario could involve a conflict between a NATO member and a non-NATO state or even between two NATO members.

Throughout the Cold War, U.S. officials constantly worried about an intra-NATO fight between ancient adversaries Greece and Turkey. About the only bond between those countries was a mutual fear of communist aggression; in nearly every other respect, they regarded each other with mutual suspicion and loathing. The persistence of Turkish claims on Greek territory, especially islands near Turkey's Adriatic coast, was—and continues to be—a potent source of friction.

Despite the Cold War incentive for solidarity against the Soviet menace, the two countries nearly came to blows on several occasions. Washington then found itself in the thankless role of trying to prevent its obstreperous allies from disrupting the alliance and playing into Moscow's hands. Matters became especially dicey in 1974 when the military junta that ruled Greece at the time staged a coup against an unacceptably moderate government in Cyprus, the nearby island nation with a Greek majority. Turkey exploited the junta's geopolitical power play by launching an invasion of Cyprus, soon occupying nearly 38 percent of the country and expelling the Greek population from the seized lands. That illegal occupation continues to this day. Washington focused on efforts to keep tensions from escalating to a full-blown war between Ankara and Athens, a task that was made easier when a chastened and more cooperative democratic government replaced the Greek junta. The United States also imposed token sanctions on Turkey for its flagrant military aggression. Within just a few years, though, U.S. officials lifted those sanctions, making it rather clear which ally they considered more important.

Tensions between Greece and Turkey remained high, and they flared again in the 1990s when the two governments backed opposite sides in the Bosnian and Kosovo civil wars. Even more than in the case of Cyprus, though, the U.S. and Turkish positions were closely aligned, while the U.S. and Greek positions conflicted. A reluctant Athens had to acquiesce to NATO military missions against its Eastern Orthodox religious brethren to support the Muslim factions that Turkey, Saudi Arabia, and other Middle East powers backed.

Still another issue that has repeatedly threatened to generate an armed conflict between Greece and Turkey is Ankara's policy of having its military aircraft routinely violate Greek airspace. That behavior is both arrogant and provocative. Thus, Washington finds itself still having to dampen the animosity between its longtime NATO partners, much as it did throughout the Cold War, only without the fear of Soviet aggression to preserve cohesion.

New Potential Snares in the Balkans

The United States has already waged two Balkan wars (in Bosnia and Kosovo) even without an alliance obligation to do so and without an allegation that an act of aggression had been committed against a NATO member. Given the language in Article 5 of the North Atlantic Treaty to regard an attack on one member as an attack on all, the likelihood of U.S. involvement in a conflict involving a NATO partner is even greater—even if the alleged aggressor is another NATO member.

Montenegro poses less of a danger of drawing the United States into a conflict involving another Balkan country than does NATO's latest invitee, Macedonia. Montenegro seems on relatively good terms with neighboring states, although it was enmeshed in an extended border dispute with Kosovo. That dispute was finally resolved in the spring of 2018 when the Kosovo parliament passed bitterly resisted legislation approving a settlement of the controversy.[5]

Macedonia, however, is on much worse terms with Kosovo and Kosovo's ethnic brethren in Albania. Officials and the populations of Kosovo and Albania have long pursued a "Greater Albania" agenda that lays claim to swaths of territory in Serbia, Montenegro, and especially Macedonia. The NATO-assisted severing of Kosovo from Serbia in 1999 was the first major triumph for that agenda, and Greater Albanian expansionists wasted no time in trying to follow up on their victory. Within months, portions of Macedonia in which ethnic Albanians constituted a majority (or in some cases, just a plurality) of the population became new arenas of instability. Ethnic Albanian leaders demanded extensive autonomy for those provinces.[6] Both the United States and its NATO allies put intense pressure on Macedonia's government to grant the demanded concessions, and Skopje reluctantly complied.

Tensions then subsided for a while, but Albanian separatist sentiments continued to fester and grow. In the past few years, a new crisis has emerged, with Albanian activists leading large anti-government demonstrations.[7] Skopje's relations with both Albania and Kosovo are showing major signs of strain. In April 2017, Macedonia's foreign ministry formally accused Albania of interfering in the country's internal political affairs. A month earlier, Macedonian president Gjorge Ivanov charged that the Albanian minority's demands were the biggest threat to his nation's sovereignty and unity.[8] Yet Washington and other Western capitals continue to press the Macedonian government to make concessions beyond those granted during the 2001 crisis. The new round of pressure is creating major splits within the Macedonian ethnic majority between moderates who are willing to try to conciliate the Albanian agitators and hardline, uncompromising nationalists.

Divisive issues continue to roil the country. The Albanian faction's demands for ever-greater autonomy keep escalating, and this caused the president and other officials to balk at making further concessions in 2018. President Ivanov dug in his heels on one key issue, repeatedly refusing to sign a new language law that would formally recognize Albanian as the primary language in certain regions of the country.[9] He and his supporters fear that such a measure would simply whet the appetite of Albanian secessionists.

The drive for a Greater Albania is gaining new momentum, and that creates major problems for a prospective NATO member. The parallels to events leading up to Kosovo's secessionist war against Serbia in the 1990s and NATO's military intervention are more than a little unsettling. It begs the question of what happens once Macedonia joins NATO if the Albanian secessionist drive does not ease but accelerates and Skopje takes action against its rebellious minority. An even worse potential problem arises if Macedonia becomes embroiled in fighting against Albania or Kosovo (or both countries) to prevent outside assistance to such a rebellion, claiming that those governments have committed aggression. The United States as NATO's leader could be drawn into such a nasty conflict.

That possibility underscores the folly of America pushing to add strategically and economically irrelevant microstates to the alliance and taking responsibility for defending them. Such "allies" are not strategic assets under any reasonable definition of the term. Instead, they are strategic liabilities and potential snares. Granted, members like Macedonia and Montenegro are not likely to involve the United States in a world war, despite Trump's inflammatory speculation. The situation in the Balkans today is not akin to the extraordinarily volatile one that existed on the eve of World War I and plunged Europe (and ultimately America) into that catastrophe. But a needless entanglement in a petty, limited armed conflict still is one entanglement too many.

The Baltic Republics as a Flashpoint

Other existing and potential NATO allies have greater potential to become tripwires for a war between the United States and Russia. That danger already exists with respect to the Baltic republics; and if NATO enthusiasts and anti-Russia hawks get their way and add Georgia or Ukraine to the alliance, the risk of such a calamity mounts.

One should not exaggerate the danger of the Baltic countries and Russia going to war, despite the hysteria in the United States and much of the West about Vladimir Putin's alleged fondness for military aggression.[10] Menacing Russian actions toward those countries have been relatively few and mild. Still, the outbreak of an armed conflict there is an ever-present danger, if not as the product of outright aggression, then as a consequence of miscalculation or disputes that spiral out of control.

An especially troubling issue is the less-than-cordial relationship between the Baltic ethnic majority populations and Russian minorities. Lithuania's population is only 9.4 percent Russian, according to that country's latest census, but both Latvia and Estonia have larger ethnic Russian minorities. In Latvia, Russian speakers make up 27 percent of the population, and in Estonia, the figure is 26 percent. The ethnic Russians tend to be concentrated in major metropolitan centers. As a result, several cities in both countries have Russian majorities. Most of that population in all three Baltic republics are the descendants of settlers that Joseph Stalin's regime imported when the USSR seized those countries at the beginning of World War II. That ugly history has fostered hostility and led to various forms of legal and social discrimination following the breakup of the USSR and the reemergence of independent Baltic nations.

The continuing discrimination against ethnic Russians is not a minor matter. Moscow has asserted a right to protect Russian minorities from abuse in all of the independent states that emerged from the wreckage of the Soviet Union.[11] That does not mean the Kremlin is itching to reconquer the Baltic republics. Even without the military risks that would exist because of the republics' membership in NATO, the political, diplomatic, and economic drawbacks to Russia of taking such a drastic step are apparent, and there is no credible evidence that Moscow intends to do so.[12] Nevertheless, the persistence of ethnic tensions is a worrisome factor that could force the hand of a Russian government at some point or serve as a pretext for aggressive action.

Either development would create an awful dilemma for the United States. As a 2016 RAND Corporation study concluded, it would be nearly impossible for NATO to defend its Baltic members against a full-scale Russian invasion for more than a few days without an extensive upgrade of the alliance's existing force deployment.[13] Washington would then face the horrid choice of either accepting the conquest of a NATO member or escalating the confrontation to the nuclear level. So again, from the standpoint of U.S. interests, it is hard to make the case that the Baltic republics are not strategic liabilities rather than assets.

Turkey: A Dangerous, Rogue Ally

The danger that Turkey could drag the United States and other NATO members into a perilous confrontation with Russia is even greater than the ability or inclination of the Baltic republics to do so. A 2015 episode highlights Ankara's willingness to engage in reckless actions that pose a danger to its alliance partners.

On November 24, 2015, a Turkish air force F-16 shot down a Russian Sukhoi Su-24 fighter near Turkey's border with Syria, killing the pilot. An especially troubling aspect of the incident was the needlessly harsh and provocative nature of the Turkish action. Evidence indicated that the Russian plane had crossed into Turkish airspace for a trivial 17 seconds.[14] Indeed, even the exact demarcation of the border between Turkey and Syria in that area is not clear. Moscow could plausibly claim that its jet was still in Syrian airspace. Since Russian air and ground forces were in Syria at the invitation of the Syrian government to help suppress the armed rebellion against President Bashar al-Assad, the presence of Russian combat aircraft on that side of the border was legitimate under international law.

Ankara's reckless belligerence was exceeded only by its hypocrisy. Turkish planes had violated the airspace of Greece more than 2,200 times in 2014 alone, and 2014 was a typical year for such incidents.[15] Greek officials have long complained that the country must devote an annoyingly large portion of its defense budget to intercepting Turkish aircraft engaging in such violations. Fortunately, though,

Athens has not adopted Turkey's apparent standard and blasted offending aircraft out of the sky.

The Turkish incident with Russia is the harbinger of potential peril. Fortunately, Vladimir Putin's government responded to the November 2015 incident with restraint, merely imposing some economic sanctions. Even those penalties proved only temporary. Talks between Putin and Turkish president Recep Tayyip Erdoğan soon produced a rapprochement between the two governments. Indeed, bilateral relations have warmed so much that U.S. leaders worry that Russia and Turkey are becoming too cozy. The growing compatibility between the two autocratic leaders eventually produced a crucial arms sale in December 2017, with Russia selling Turkey S-400 air defense missiles over Washington's objections.[16]

Given the bilateral rapprochement since the 2015 crisis, worries about war between Turkey and Russia might seem irrelevant. Yet as events throughout history have demonstrated, circumstances can change quickly, and nations on friendly terms one moment can become staunch adversaries the next. The 2015 incident still highlights disturbing issues about Turkey's behavior and the Article 5 obligation to regard an attack on one NATO member as an attack on all. The risks entailed in that obligation multiply as the number of members increases. Maintaining a commitment to defend the relatively stable nations of Western Europe during the Cold War is one thing—although the tensions between Greece and Turkey indicate the problems involved with even those obligations. Doing so on behalf of nearly twice that number of NATO countries, some of which are far less stable and predictable, is more perilous.

Even the task of sorting out which party to a conflict is the aggressor is not always easy. For example, it was far from clear whether the 2015 incident was a case of Russian aggression or a clumsy Turkish overreaction and provocation. Yet if Russia had responded to the downing of its plane by launching strikes against the Turkish missile batteries, it is a safe bet that Ankara would have demanded that its NATO partners, especially the United States, help repel such "aggression"—despite the potentially dire consequences of escalating a conflict with a nuclear-armed adversary. Wise American leaders should be wary of alliance commitments that enable any supposed ally to put the republic in such a quandary.

Even Greater Risks with New Allies in Russia's Neighborhood

Washington's alliance commitments to such countries as Turkey and the Baltic states already expose the United States to worrisome military risks with respect to a nuclear-armed Russia. The admission of Georgia or Ukraine to NATO would be even more reckless. Yet U.S. leaders have long sought alliance membership for both countries.

A 2007 report by Human Rights Watch was notably critical of Georgia's human rights abuses despite the governing regime's professions of respect for democratic values. But the report also noted that U.S. leaders viewed Georgia "as a small but crucial bulwark to counter Russian dominance in the region and as an important ally for the United States."[17] Seeing Georgia as a potential NATO security partner meant that U.S. officials were willing to overlook the Georgian government's rather sketchy human rights record. As for Ukraine, American policymakers already saw that country as an even more essential asset in the effort to contain Moscow's power.

President George W. Bush enthusiastically embraced the ambitions of both countries for NATO membership.[18] As discussed in Chapter 2, that was an ambitious step that France, Germany, and several of Washington's other alliance partners were unwilling to take when Bush formally proposed the first stage in that process, the Membership Action Plan, for Georgia and Ukraine, at the NATO summit in April 2008.[19]

The potential danger to both the United States and its major European allies of undertaking security obligations to volatile new members became all too evident when war broke out between Moscow and Tbilisi in August 2008. Indeed, even before the outbreak of that conflict, ample signs warned that the Georgian government was a political and military loose cannon.

The international conduct of Georgia's ostensibly democratic president, Mikheil Saakashvili, who came to power during that country's 2003 "Rose Revolution," should have warned his American sponsors.

Secretary of Defense Robert Gates aptly described him as "an impetuous Georgian nationalist" who went out of his way to push the envelope on sensitive issues.[20] Other U.S. leaders and Western news media accounts, though, largely ignored signs of Saakashvili's risky behavior. That wishful thinking persisted even when his actions helped trigger a war between Georgia and Russia. Instead, Georgia's Western admirers portrayed the conflict as a case of blatant Russian aggression. President Bush concluded, "It was clear that the Russians couldn't stand a democratic Georgia with a pro-Western president."[21]

The reality was more complex, and responsibility for the war was murkier than Bush and other hawks suggested. Indeed, Saakashvili took the fatal aggressive step when he launched a military operation into the secessionist region of South Ossetia. Russian peacekeeping forces had been deployed in that region since disorder erupted following the dissolution of the Soviet Union in 1991. On the heels of Georgia's declaration of independence earlier that year, South Ossetia and another region, Abkhazia, sought to break away and establish independent states. Influential Russians encouraged such secessionist sentiments. The simmering violence in Georgia escalated to civil war, which would not subside until late 1993. The deployment of Russian peacekeeping forces during the conflict ultimately made both regions Moscow's de facto protectorates.

Saakashvili fumed at having two significant portions of Georgia lie beyond the authority of his government. In early August 2008, he responded to one of the periodic cross-border shelling incidents with Ossetian units by launching a major operation, apparently with the goal of reestablishing control over the breakaway region. Unfortunately, Saakashvili's offensive also inflicted casualties on the Russian peacekeeping force. Moscow responded with a full-scale counteroffensive that soon led to the occupation of several Georgian cities and brought Russian troops to the outskirts of the capital, Tbilisi.

In retrospect, Saakashvili acted rashly, even irresponsibly. He may well have expected NATO, and especially the United States as the alliance's leader, to come to Georgia's aid militarily. Such an expectation would not have been unfounded, given Washington's incessant praise for Georgian democracy in general and his government in particular.

The United States also had supplied Georgia with millions of dollars in weaponry and provided training to Georgian troops.[22]

Nevertheless, the Bush administration wisely backed away from the abyss of a military confrontation with Russia. When Bush called Saakashvili just hours after the commencement of the Russian offensive, the Georgian president urged him not to abandon a fellow democracy. Bush assured him of Washington's commitment to Georgia's territorial integrity, but tellingly stopped short of pledging military backing.[23] In a telephone call to Saakashvili, the habitually hawkish John McCain would famously intone that "today, we are all Georgians."[24] But U.S. and NATO forces remained in their barracks. Confronted with unexpected U.S. restraint, Georgia had to sue for a humiliating cease fire and de facto peace with its large neighbor.

It is sobering, though, to consider what might have happened if the European powers had acquiesced to Washington's wishes and given Georgia membership in NATO. Under Article 5, the United States and its allies would have been obligated to consider an attack on Georgia as an attack on them all. Since the allied governments accused Russia of aggression (despite the conflicting evidence), they might have had little choice but to come to Tbilisi's aid, regardless of the risks. Even the mere possibility should be a cautionary lesson to Washington about the perils of backing a small, volatile client state like Georgia.

Yet some advocates of NATO expansion seem to have learned the opposite lesson. Bush later mused, "I wonder if they [the Russians] would have been as aggressive if NATO had approved Georgia's [Membership Action Plan] application."[25] Proponents of a U.S-led NATO tend to have excessive faith in the supposed infallibility of deterrence, but Bush's comment takes that faith to a whole new level. He was arguing that Moscow would have been deterred not only if Georgia had been a full NATO member enjoying the Article 5 guarantee, but even if the country merely had been approved for the first stage of possible admission. Bush seems to believe that the latter action might have been enough to intimidate Putin. To put it mildly, that notion is implausible.

Given its size, Ukraine would appear to constitute a more serious, substantive strategic asset for the United States. But extending NATO membership to that country would entail even greater risks than giving that status to Georgia. Even without Ukraine becoming a formal NATO member, Washington's relationship to Kiev increasingly is that of de facto military allies, and such a flirtation is profoundly unwise. In addition to the participation of U.S. units in provocative NATO military exercises with Ukrainian forces, Washington's military collaboration with Kiev is expanding on multiple fronts. Recent measures provoked Moscow further, and they entangled the United States to an unwise extent with an extremely murky, ideologically troubling Ukrainian regime.

President Trump's secretary of defense, James Mattis, acknowledged in February 2018 that U.S. instructors were training Ukrainian military units at a base in western Ukraine.[26] Washington also has approved two important arms sales to Kiev's ground forces since December 2017. The initial transaction was limited to small arms, which at least could be portrayed as purely defensive weapons. That agreement involved the export of model M107A1 sniper systems, ammunition, and associated parts and accessories, a sale valued at $41.5 million.

An April 2018 transaction was more serious and substantive. Not only was it larger ($47 million), it included far more lethal weaponry, especially 210 Javelin anti-tank missiles—the kind of weapons that Barack Obama's administration had declined to give Kiev out of concern that such aid might unduly provoke Moscow.[27] Russian officials were quite displeased with the first sale; they were livid about the second one.[28] Moreover, in May, Congress passed legislation that authorized $250 million in military assistance, including lethal weaponry, to Ukraine. Congress had twice voted for military support on a similar scale during the last years of Obama's administration, but the White House had blocked implementation. The Trump administration cleared that obstacle out of the way in December 2017 at the same time that it approved the initial small-weapons sale. The passage of the May 2018 legislation means that the path is now open for a dramatic escalation of U.S. military backing for Kiev.

On September 1, 2018, former U.S. ambassador to NATO, Kurt Volker, disclosed during an interview with the *Guardian* that Washington's future military aid to Kiev would likely include weapons sales to

Ukraine's air force and navy as well as the army.[29] "The Javelins are mainly symbolic and it's not clear if they would ever be used," Aric Toler, a research scholar at the staunchly pro-NATO, anti-Russia Atlantic Council, asserted. One could well dispute his sanguine conclusion, but even Toler conceded, "Support for the Ukrainian navy and air defence would be a big deal. That would be far more significant."[30]

Volker's cavalier attitude about U.S. arms sales to a country locked in a crisis with Russia epitomizes the arrogance and tone-deaf views that too many U.S. foreign policy officials exhibit regarding the sensitive Ukraine issue. He insisted, "We can have a conversation with Ukraine like we would with any other country about what do they need. I think that there's going to be some discussion about naval capability because as you know their navy was basically taken by Russia [when the Soviet Union dissolved]. And so they need to rebuild a navy and they have very limited air capability as well. I think we'll have to look at air defence." Such a stance is very close to how Washington would treat a NATO member.

Calls for closer U.S. and NATO cooperation with Kiev escalated after a November 2018 incident between Ukrainian and Russian warships in the Kerch Strait. The strait, which connects the Black Sea and the Sea of Azov, separates Russia's Taman Peninsula from the Crimea Peninsula. Despite Moscow's annexation of the latter in 2014, Kiev still considers Crimea to be Ukrainian territory, a position that the United States and its allies back emphatically. Moreover, passage through the strait is the only maritime link between Ukraine's Black Sea ports and ports on the Azov. Kiev views the strait as international waters and relies on a 2003 bilateral navigation treaty to vindicate its position.

With the annexation of Crimea, however, Russia now regards the waterway as its territorial waters. When three Ukrainian ships violated Moscow's demand for 48 hours' notice and official permission for transit (a procedure Kiev had followed a few months earlier), Russian security forces intervened, ramming one ship and firing on the others, wounding several Ukrainian sailors and then seizing the offending vessels.[31]

The United States and the other NATO members reacted with fury to this incident. NATO held an emergency meeting with the Ukrainian government. NATO Secretary General Jens Stoltenberg pledged the alliance's "full support for Ukraine's territorial integrity and sovereignty, including its full navigational rights in its territorial waters under international law."[32] Ukraine's leaders wanted far more than NATO's moral support, however. In an interview with the German publication *Bild*, President Petro Poroshenko expressed the hope that NATO members "are now ready to relocate naval ships to the Sea of Azov in order to assist Ukraine and provide security."[33]

Leaving aside the problem that much of the Sea of Azov is too shallow (in some portions no more than six meters deep) to accommodate most NATO warships, attempting to use the Kerch Strait without Moscow's permission would create a horrifically dangerous crisis. Even moving NATO ships to the eastern waters of the Black Sea adjacent to the strait would constitute a reckless provocation. Unfortunately, some political leaders, media figures, and policy experts were pushing the latter step even before the Kerch Strait incident.[34]

There were now even louder cries for an increase in measures to show resolve and strengthen security ties between NATO and Kiev. Rep. Eliot Engel (D-NY), who became chair of the House Foreign Affairs Committee in the next Congress, urged an increase in U.S. arms sales to Ukraine, asserting, "If Putin starts seeing Russian soldier fatalities, that changes his equation." Senate Armed Services Committee chair James Inhofe (R-OK) threatened new sanctions on Russia and called for a coordinated response between the United States and its European allies. "If Putin continues his Black Sea bullying," Inhofe stated, "the United States and Europe must consider imposing additional sanctions on Russia, inserting a greater U.S. and NATO presence in the Black Sea region and increasing military assistance for Ukraine." Sen. Robert Menendez (D-NJ) echoed those views. Menendez called for tougher sanctions, additional NATO exercises on the Black Sea, and more security aid to Ukraine, "including lethal maritime equipment and weapons."[35]

Even before the Kerch Strait episode, Kiev was vigorously lobbying for more military aid from the United States, and Washington appeared quite receptive to that appeal. U.S. and Ukrainian officials were in "close discussion" regarding the possibility Washington would supply another tranche of powerful weapons for Kiev's fight in eastern Ukraine, Ukrainian Foreign Minister Pavlo Klimkin told reporters on November 18, 2018, a day after he met with U.S. Secretary of State Mike Pompeo in Washington.[36] That was a week before the Kerch Strait clash, and the timing of the latter should have raised suspicions about it being a pretext for a policy that Kiev and Washington intended to adopt.

Indeed, Poroshenko, with his political fortunes flagging ahead of a spring 2019 presidential election, seized on the Kerch Strait incident to proclaim martial law in 10 regions—areas of the country that tended to be hostile to him and his party. Poroshenko also paraded around the country in full military uniform, apparently hoping to ride a surge of patriotic and anti-Russian sentiment to electoral victory. His strategy failed, and he suffered a landslide loss to a political newcomer—Ukraine's leading comedian, Volodymyr Zelensky.

Trump administration officials have taken a rather cavalier attitude toward U.S. security cooperation with a country that is not averse to provoking its larger neighbor. Worse, Washington does not seem to have abandoned its hope that the major European allies will eventually relent and let Ukraine join NATO—a step that would significantly increase Washington's obligations and risks. At present, that result seems unlikely, owing to the seemingly unyielding opposition of several allied governments, especially Germany, to enlarging the alliance to include Georgia and Ukraine (see Chapter 3). In adopting that position, Berlin and its cautious colleagues may be saving Washington from its own folly.

America's NATO Commitments Now Entail Far More Risks than Benefits

The first question that U.S. leaders should ask about any alliance commitment is whether the ally is even worth risking a sacrifice of American treasure and lives. Does that country have great strategic or economic significance to the United States? Risking war to defend another country ought to be no casual matter. A military alliance with such a profound obligation is not akin to an economic or social association. The obligation is deadly serious—and U.S. policymakers must never adopt the flippant attitude that because the United States is powerful, it can undertake virtually any commitment, confident that no adversary will ever be daring (or reckless) enough to challenge it. The history of international affairs is littered with examples of deterrence failures on the part of great powers attempting to protect allies and clients.

Washington's implicit assumption is that neither Russia nor any other country would dare challenge the Article 5 commitment. Foreign policy should never be based on a bluff. Yet for the United States, the obligation to regard an attack on any NATO member (no matter how insignificant) as an attack on America itself potentially puts the very existence of the republic at risk. If deterrence ever failed, especially if the challenger were Russia, Washington would face the choice between a bad option and a horrific one. The former would entail reneging on a solemn treaty commitment to a NATO ally, thereby raising major doubts about U.S. credibility. The latter would mean going to war against a power armed with more than 2,000 nuclear weapons and risking mutual annihilation. Smart great powers don't put themselves in such a position.

Doing so is especially unwise if the ally being defended is not utterly essential to America's own security. Even during the Cold War, the wisdom of embracing that level of risk was questionable. However, Europe was by far the main strategic and economic prize during that era, and the United States faced not just a geopolitical challenger, but a messianic, totalitarian, expansionist power. Keeping democratic Europe out of Moscow's orbit arguably justified undertaking a high level of risk. The Kremlin's expansionist ambitions may have never actually extended that far, especially given the headaches it repeatedly encountered trying to control Eastern Europe, but U.S. leaders were understandably wary of taking the chance. A Soviet Union in control of populous, economically powerful Western Europe would have made for a very uncomfortable U.S. status in the resulting international system. Still, reasonable critics might contend that playing nuclear chicken with Moscow was excessively perilous, even for such important geostrategic stakes.

Whatever the merits of incurring that level of risk to shield major strategic and economic assets such as Britain, France, Italy, and (West) Germany, those considerations no longer apply. Russia is a conventional, regional power—not a totalitarian state with global expansionist objectives. Equally important, most NATO members added since the end of the Cold War are not even remotely considered major powers. The vast majority are not even meaningful allies, but weak security dependents. Risking national suicide to protect such modest, indeed mostly trivial, clients is the essence of foreign policy folly.

Beyond determining whether an ally is worth the risk of going to war, there could well be another difficult decisionmaking problem if a crisis erupted. As noted, determining whether the alliance partner is victim or aggressor might be difficult. The incident with Turkey confirmed the problem, but clashes involving other countries could raise similar issues.

Continuing, much less increasing, the forward deployment of U.S. military forces intensifies the risks that the rigid security commitment to the NATO allies already entails. It is especially imprudent to station troops, tanks, warplanes, and missiles in NATO's eastern members near the Russian frontier (or to maintain a disguised ongoing deployment via constantly rotating "temporary" deployments).

Even a minor incident could instantly engulf forward-deployed U.S. military units in combat, effectively foreclosing Washington's policy options. Indeed, that is why those members want the U.S. deployments. Daniel Szeligowski, a senior research fellow at the Polish Institute for International Affairs, emphasizes that benefit to his country and its neighbors: "From the Polish perspective, the deployment of U.S. troops to Poland and Baltic states means a real deterrence since it increases the probability of the U.S. forces engagement in case of potential aggression from Russia."[37]

The Trump administration may be inclined to dispense with the fiction that constant rotational deployments of U.S. forces in East European countries do not constitute a permanent military presence. During a state visit to Washington in September 2018, Poland's president, Andrzej Duda, promised to provide $2 billion toward the construction if the United States built a base in his country. Duda even offered to name the base "Fort Trump" in a transparent appeal to the U.S. president's notorious vanity. "Poland is willing to make a very major contribution to the United States to come in and have a presence in Poland," Trump said in the Oval Office. "If they're willing to do that, it's something we will certainly talk about." He added that the United States would take Duda's proposal "very seriously."[38]

The *American Conservative*'s Daniel Larison warned that putting a U.S. base in Poland "would further antagonize Russia, and it would create one more overseas military installation that the U.S. doesn't need to have. Trump is often accused of wanting to 'retreat' from the world, but his willingness to entertain this proposal shows that he doesn't care about stationing U.S. forces abroad so long as someone else is footing most of the bill."[39] Larison's comment underscores how the potential deleterious impact of Washington's NATO commitments goes far beyond simple burden-sharing grievances. The cost issue would be the least of the problems created by establishing an official, permanent U.S. military presence in a state on Russia's border, encroaching on Moscow's military bastion, Kaliningrad. The rotating deployments are bad enough, but ostentatiously building a major base would escalate that provocation.

Playing Thermonuclear Russian Roulette

Extending U.S. security guarantees to NATO allies was risky enough during the Cold War when major geopolitical stakes were involved. If deterrence had failed, a confrontation with the USSR could have escalated and culminated in a thermonuclear exchange, causing millions of American casualties and possibly extinguishing America as a functioning society. There was always the danger that a Kremlin leader would conclude that the U.S. pledge under Article 5 was a bluff and make the fateful decision to challenge Washington's willingness to risk the American population on behalf of allies. Fortunately, the Soviet dictators were not inclined to be Hitler-style gamblers, and they never put the Article 5 commitment to the test. Despite some close calls on both sides with early warning systems giving false signals about a possible launch of enemy missiles, no disastrous accidents occurred for that reason either.[40] But it is appropriate to acknowledge that the Cold War could have had a far more tragic ending. Keeping U.S. missiles on hair-trigger alert seems extremely reckless absent the vicious rivalry with the USSR.

U.S. leaders relied on the assumption that the geostrategic assets at stake were large and important enough that extended deterrence to cover Western Europe was inherently credible to the Kremlin and would not be challenged. The assumption proved valid in the Cold War context. Even if the Soviets (and the West Europeans) may have wondered from time to time if Washington's professed willingness to commit national suicide to prevent the Red Army from conquering Europe was genuine, no rational person wanted to test that proposition.

In today's world, however, the inherent believability of the U.S. pledge is weaker. A vow to incur even grave risks to prevent a totalitarian superpower enemy from dominating such key international economic and strategic assets as Britain, France, Germany, and Italy had a reasonable degree of credibility. But the notion that the United States would honor such a security pledge to prevent a conventional, conservative regional power like post-Soviet Russia from reasserting imperial control over one or more weak neighboring states strains credulity to the breaking point. America's risks under Article 5 are at least as great as they were during the Cold War, while the stakes involved—and the benefits to America of retaining a bloated roster of allies—are much less.

The intrinsically weaker credibility of extended deterrence under these new circumstances cannot be overcome by pounding the table or increasing the number and intensity of America's security pledges to NATO allies. But NATO partisans blindly refuse to acknowledge that reality. Former U.S. ambassador to NATO Ivo H. Daalder, for example, argues that "the biggest threat today is not a deliberate war, as it was [in the Cold War], but the possibility of miscalculation. One worry is that Russia might not believe that NATO would actually come to the defense of its most exposed allies—which is why strong statements of reassurance and commitment by all NATO countries, and not least the United States, are so vital." Daalder even puts the verbal aspect on the same plane as tangible military deployments. The forward presence of NATO forces is an important signal of resolve, he states, "but they need to be backed by words that leave no doubt of the intention to use these forces to defend allies if they are attacked."[41]

Daalder misses the crucial point: a potential adversary will more likely judge the credibility of a deterrence pledge based on the importance of the tangible interests at stake to the guarantor power compared to the risks the power incurs. Simply repeating assurances that "we really mean it" will not make a possible challenger believe an implausible guarantee. Washington's problem today is that promising to risk national suicide for small allies that have little economic or strategic importance looks like a bluff—one that Moscow may call in the midst of a crisis, if Russian leaders believe their country's vital interests are at stake. That is why expanding NATO and adding an assortment of marginally relevant, volatile dependents in Russia's immediate neighborhood merely weakens the credibility of Washington's long-standing security guarantee to more significant alliance partners farther west. Daalder's emphasis on the need to repeat and emphasize the sanctity of the U.S. pledge to all European allies suggests just how much he and other NATO defenders worry that otherwise a Kremlin leader might call that bluff.

The greater disparity between risks and benefits virtually invites a challenge at some point. Despite the overwrought propaganda in much of the Western media about Putin being the new Hitler, his behavior indicates that he is a prudent risk taker, not a reckless one. But one of the worst aspects of a permanent military alliance is that it is permanent. We must assume that unknown Russian leaders a decade or a generation from now will not be gamblers. The questionable notion that the United States is really willing to risk thermonuclear war to protect minuscule states in Russia's neighborhood or on Russia's border itself must be reconsidered. It is an extremely imprudent assumption and a high-stakes bet on Washington's part.

Moreover, the willingness of current U.S. leaders to placate NATO's East European members by stationing American troops and warplanes and establishing permanent bases on their soil increases the likelihood of a future tragedy. The goal of European governments, now as during the Cold War, is to deny U.S. policymakers the element of choice about America becoming embroiled in any conflict that breaks out. U.S. forces there serve as tripwires to guarantee that Washington must honor the Article 5 pledge, even if doing so is self-destructive folly. The underlying perverse logic of insisting on U.S. tripwire forces is that the Kremlin, believing that the United States will have no choice but to intervene on behalf of an ally if American troops are among the initial casualties in a conflict, will never take the fateful first step of attacking a NATO member, even a small, vulnerable one. By collaborating in this denial of policy choice, American officials are engaging in the geostrategic equivalent of making a huge wager on one turn of the roulette wheel—except in this case, the lives of millions of Americans are at stake, rather than mere dollars. It is a foolish and irresponsible bet.

Secretary of State Henry Kissinger reportedly once observed that great powers do not commit suicide on behalf of allies. But he should have said that great powers do not *willingly* commit suicide on behalf of allies. As the cataclysmic descent into war by Europe's rival blocs in 1914 demonstrated, great powers sometimes do end up, however inadvertently, committing suicide on behalf of allies. Washington must adopt important policy changes to make certain that America does not stumble into a similar tragedy in the 21st century.

CHAPTER 5

U.S. PATERNALISM STIFLES INDEPENDENT EUROPEAN SECURITY CAPABILITIES

Current NATO policy implicitly continues to regard even the alliance's major European members as little more than glorified U.S. security dependents rather than robust, capable powers. The United States has kept a tight rein on alliance military strategy since the beginning. It is no accident that NATO's top military post, Supreme Allied Commander Europe (SACEUR), has always been an American officer. A European has always been given the post of Secretary General, the alliance's top diplomat. Being Secretary General certainly is more than a purely ceremonial post, but (especially in a crisis) SACEUR and U.S. leaders in Washington hold the real decisionmaking power.

The insistence on U.S. preeminence was apparent throughout the Cold War, and it did not change appreciably when the Cold War ended. Washington's seizure of leadership in dealing with the Balkan crises in the 1990s made clear that U.S. leaders had little confidence in the ability of their European allies to deal independently even with a secondary, subregional disruption of the security environment. Nor did Washington welcome any evidence to the contrary. As discussed in Chapter 1, both George H. W. Bush's and Bill Clinton's administrations displayed contempt for and quietly undermined what limited initiatives the Europeans did undertake to manage the problems associated with the unraveling of Yugoslavia. That attitude was especially apparent regarding the initial European initiatives to resolve the ethnic confrontations in Bosnia-Herzegovina.

Despite the Clinton foreign policy team's feigned official reluctance to have Washington take the leadership reins during the Bosnia situation, U.S. leaders firmly grabbed those reins to affirm the allegedly imperative need for continued American leadership of the transatlantic security relationship. Indeed, the same determination was evident in Washington's overall global posture. In 1998, Secretary of State Madeleine Albright stated explicitly that "we are the indispensable nation. We stand tall and we see further than other countries into the future. . . ."[1] Albright may have been a bit more brazen and undiplomatic (if not downright arrogant) than most of her colleagues in the American foreign policy establishment, but she accurately reflected their views.

Washington's negative reactions to periodic European suggestions that the European Union undertake a security role as well as its traditional economic role reflect both America's insecurity about its status as the indispensable power and its determination to maintain a hegemonic role. For decades, U.S. leaders have viewed suggestions of strengthening any competing European institution with barely concealed hostility. Early potential competitors during the post–Cold War years included the Western European Union and the Conference on Security and Cooperation in Europe (later the Organization for Security and Cooperation in Europe). Brent Scowcroft, George H. W. Bush's national security adviser, gave a candid U.S. reaction to the position that the French government adopted following Moscow's acceptance of Germany's reunification and the membership of a united Germany in NATO. French president Francois Mitterrand, he contended, "appeared to believe, or hope, that NATO would atrophy as the instrument of European security, with political stability increasingly supplied by the [Western European Union and Conference on Security and Cooperation in Europe]."[2]

Scowcroft was not at all pleased with Mitterrand's apparent views, and nearly all U.S. policymakers in the Bush I, Clinton, and Bush II administrations shared his uneasiness and hostility. Jolyon Howorth, the Jean Monnet Professor at the University of Bath (UK), and John T. S. Keeler,

University of Pittsburgh professor of political science, argue that early on in the post–Cold War period, the European governments manifested "independence bordering on insubordination," chafing under Washington's continued domination of transatlantic security relations.[3] Despite the somewhat humiliating experience resulting from tepid European attempts to manage the Bosnia turmoil, the restlessness actually deepened as the decade went on.

More substantive manifestations of growing European assertiveness regarding security issues took place in 1999. At summits in January and December of that year, NATO's European members pushed for the adoption of a European Security and Defense Policy (ESDP). The ESDP grew out of the earlier European Security and Defense Initiative (ESDI), which Washington had found little cause to oppose. The ESDI was a classic burden-sharing scheme, in which the Europeans promised to do more in the security arena by creating a stronger "European pillar" within NATO. But the latter point was the crucial caveat: an increased European security role was to occur only within the strict confines of NATO.

Even then, NATO's new Strategic Concept, approved at the 50th anniversary summit in April 1999, showed continuing divisions regarding the alliance's proper mission and the appropriate role of ESDI. Much of the language in the final document was an awkward compromise between U.S. (and British) policymakers who insisted on continued undisputed NATO primacy and officials in other European countries who sought greater latitude for security initiatives outside of the alliance.

One key paragraph practically oozed with primacist language. It praised the European members for having made decisions "to enable them to assume greater responsibilities in the security and defense field," but it immediately stressed that the ESDI would be developed "within NATO." Another especially convoluted passage sought to balance virtually every conceivable objective of both camps. ESDI would "reinforce the transatlantic partnership"; yet it would also enable the European allies to "act by themselves" in certain (unspecified) situations. However, they could act by themselves only "as required through the readiness of the Alliance, on a case-by-case basis, and by consensus, to make its [NATO's] assets and capabilities available for operations in which the Alliance is not engaged militarily."[4]

The ESDP that evolved from the ESDI promised to be much more worrisome to U.S. officials committed to maintaining the NATO status quo and U.S. dominance.[5] With the ESDP, the European countries seemed to be contemplating serious, autonomous, or perhaps fully independent initiatives in the security arena.

Stifling European Security Initiatives and Preserving U.S. Hegemony

Whenever proposals to establish even a modest independent European security mechanism have surfaced, U.S. officials and their ideological allies in the American foreign policy community have moved to shoot down such ideas. Washington's reaction to the ESDP was quite revealing. Texas A&M University professor Christopher Layne concludes that ESDP was "envisioned as the backbone of an independent European security policy, one developed by Europeans without U.S. input." If that was not enough to unsettle U.S. leaders, Layne writes, "at their November 2000 meeting the EU's defense ministers gave ESDP concrete expression by announcing plans to create a sixty-thousand-strong Rapid Reaction Force (RRF)."[6]

The ESDP and RRF plans triggered an intense disagreement between the United States and the EU about how far the "Europeanization" of the Continent's defense could or should go. Tensions escalated in late 2000 when French president Jacques Chirac and prime minister Lionel Jospin emphasized that, although the RRF would draw on some European military units also assigned to NATO, it would be an autonomous European force. They indicated further that it would be the embryo of an EU army with a chain of command, headquarters, and staff entirely separate from NATO.[7]

Layne notes that the U.S. reaction to the RRF was "swift and hostile." There was also an element of panic. Speaking to the NATO defense ministers meeting in Brussels in December 2000, Secretary of

Defense William Cohen warned that if the EU created a defense capability outside of NATO, the alliance would become "a relic of the past."[8] Pentagon leaders privately discussed having Washington threaten the European allies that the United States would withdraw its own forces from Europe if the EU created the RRF without embedding it firmly in NATO.[9]

John Bolton—who would become a senior policy official in George W. Bush's administration and, later, President Trump's national security adviser—excoriated the RRF as "a dagger pointed at NATO's heart."[10] Washington's countermove soon became, and has consistently remained, a concerted campaign to sabotage any notion of a separate European rapid response force and to develop a similar capability under NATO. The conceptual roots of the NATO Response Force began in the early years of the 21st century with Washington's effort to thwart the creation of a purely European version.

The plan to develop the NATO Response Force confirmed that the Bush administration was just as committed as its predecessor to diverting European defense efforts and resources away from the ESDP and RRF. Layne is correct that for all the talk of burden sharing, the United States has never desired a truly equal, much less autonomous, democratic Europe when it comes to security matters. "U.S. policymakers' reaction to ESDP and the RRF," he contends, reflected "longstanding U.S. fears that an equal and independent Europe would throw off Washington's tutelage." The reaction also reflected Washington's pervasive suspicion that the ESDP and RRF were "the 'camel's nose under the tent'"—that they would "become rivals to NATO in European security affairs."[11]

The Clinton administration's policy demands regarding the ESDP certainly indicated an insistence on maintaining NATO's preeminence—and, therefore, Washington's domination of Europe's security architecture. The administration's approach was based on the "three Ds" that ESDP or any new security initiative must reflect: that is, a new program must not *diminish* NATO's role, *duplicate* NATO's capabilities, or *discriminate* against any NATO members that did not belong to the EU.[12] Not surprisingly, the administration believed that the ESDP violated all of those strictures.

Officials in the subsequent Bush administration exhibited a similar attitude. In October 2003, Nicholas Burns, the U.S. ambassador to NATO, sharply criticized the EU's plan to develop an independent military capacity. Burns branded that effort as "one of the greatest dangers to the transatlantic community."[13] Condoleezza Rice, national security adviser in George W. Bush's first term and secretary of state in his second, noted that British prime minister Tony Blair sought to "get a nod" from the president that the United States would support the creation of "enhanced independent European forces." Blair's request constituted a significant shift in London's position. Previously, Britain had been at least as insistent as the United States that all defense measures be implemented through NATO. Bush did not explicitly reject Blair's overture, but he worried that the Europeans might "hollow out NATO" by trying to get their "meager forces to do double duty."[14]

The Bush administration's response to the RRF, like that of its predecessor, indicated little receptivity to a more vigorous European commitment of forces if that step occurred outside of NATO. That continuing resistance underscored the self-serving, rather hypocritical nature of the U.S. calls for greater burden sharing. Washington's countermove to the ESDP and the RRF was to propose creating a military response force within NATO. U.S. officials lobbied intensely for that option, and eventually, France and other powers who favored a European-controlled rapid reaction capability capitulated. The NATO version went into operation in 2003, and it has taken on new relevance—especially as tensions grow between the alliance and Russia.

Washington's negative view of "Europeans only" security proposals has not diminished in the intervening years. Even Trump's demands for greater European seriousness about collective defense emphasize greater financial burden sharing and a willingness to do more to support NATO's overall defense efforts. There are few, if any, indications that Washington is even willing to share decisionmaking authority within NATO, much less that U.S. leaders would look kindly on the creation of new European security arrangements that exclude the United States.

Moreover, one reason for Washington's insistence on expanding NATO's membership was the perception that most of the drive to implement ESDP came from France and other countries in "old Europe." Secretary of Defense Rumsfeld and other Bush administration officials believed that Central and Eastern European nations were extremely grateful to the United States for standing firm against the Soviet Union throughout the Cold War and eventually liberating the satellite nations. U.S. policymakers were confident that those new NATO (and EU) members would willingly embrace Washington's continued leadership.

Rumsfeld's comment dividing democratic Europe into two distinct categories came in response to a reporter's observation that the "mood among European allies" was not supportive of using military force against Iraq. But it applied to more than the Bush administration's Iraq policy. "You're thinking of Europe as Germany and France," Rumsfeld replied scornfully. "I don't. I think that's old Europe." He then argued that given the expansion of NATO membership and the imminent prospect of more expansion, the alliance's center of gravity had shifted east. Those countries, Rumsfeld asserted, are "not with France and Germany on this, they're with the United States."[15] And he was correct. Ten East European countries, most of which would soon join NATO, promptly rejected the French-German position regarding Iraq and endorsed the U.S. stance of pursuing military action if deemed necessary.

U.S. leaders were already applying a similar strategy of mobilizing their accommodating East European allies to deal with internal NATO and even EU issues. If the United States expressed opposition to the creation of independent EU security entities, American officials were confident that the countries of "new Europe" would endorse Washington's policy preferences, rather than those of Paris or Berlin. For the most part, that expectation seems to have been borne out; the Central and East European nations have been content with, even enthusiastic about, the continuation of U.S. hegemony. In his memoirs, Rumsfeld contends that he meant to say "old NATO," rather than "old Europe," as though the impact of the latter term would have been much different, but his broader reasoning was apparent. Extending NATO membership, he conceded, already had a very important effect. "This shift in the center of gravity of NATO eastward naturally reduced the role of France and Germany." And Rumsfeld was perfectly happy with that development.[16]

Washington's drive to strangle the ESDP and RRF succeeded in the near term—although as discussed below, plans to create an effective and independent European security mechanism are showing signs of renewed life. In the meantime, the U.S. determination to preserve its hegemony in Europe at all costs has needlessly increased America's defense burdens and risks. Insisting on perpetuating Europe's security dependence is not a wise policy in the 21st century—if it ever was.

The fault for the perpetuation of an obsolete transatlantic security relationship does not reside entirely with the United States. True, U.S. leaders have manifested their displeasure every time European officials floated trial balloons about the EU undertaking independent security responsibilities. But allied governments have backed off without much of a struggle every time as well. Moreover, despite periodic signs of greater assertiveness and expressed desires for more meaningful policy autonomy since the end of the Cold War, the Europeans themselves have failed to exercise sustained leadership at key moments when opportunities have arisen. The Clinton administration undermined initial European efforts to manage the Bosnian crisis, for example, but leading EU countries did not mount much of a resistance to Washington's attempts at meddling and its usurpation of leadership.

Sometimes, the European members of NATO have seemed almost as willing to relinquish leadership roles and responsibilities as the Americans have been to continue emphasizing a dominant U.S. role. The unhealthy relationship of patron and dependent that developed during the Cold War, initially out of necessity, has persisted. Even during the early years of the post–Cold War period when the sense of relief at the Soviet Union's disintegration was at its zenith, European elites as well as their American counterparts were determined to honor NATO Secretary General Lord Ismay's admonition about "keeping the Americans in," even if it might no longer be necessary to "keep the Russians out" or "the Germans down."

The Europeans remain committed to the objective of retaining the American military presence and defense shield, even when they profess to want more independent security capabilities. In other words, they have wanted the best of both worlds: greater policy autonomy, but continued U.S. protection. That balancing act has proven to be quite difficult because U.S. leaders insist on both greater European burden sharing within NATO and continued deference to U.S. leadership and policy preferences.

Indeed, the European allies find themselves under pressure to mute their objections even to U.S. policies that they fear are ill-advised to avoid any risk that the United States might decide to make its role on the Continent a lower priority. That point became evident with George W. Bush's determination to invade and occupy Iraq to oust Saddam Hussein. With the exception of British prime minister Tony Blair, leaders of most other key NATO members were very uneasy about the U.S. decision. Although some ultimately did provide tepid endorsements, Germany and other countries refused to provide forces for the mission. The European lack of enthusiasm for Bush's crusade was palpable because, among other reasons, they feared (correctly) that Washington's regime-change war would cause more turmoil and violence in Iraq and the rest of the Middle East. The spillover from such turbulence inevitably would have a major negative impact on Europe.

Nevertheless, the NATO allies did not challenge Washington's Iraq policy in a serious manner. European governments have been careful not to offend the United States on other issues as well, such as the open-ended war in Afghanistan or backing the Saudi-led war in Yemen. Even the European resistance to the Trump administration's relentlessly hostile policy toward Iran has remained carefully measured. Germany and France did refuse to follow Trump's lead when he repudiated the Joint Comprehensive Plan of Action that the United States and other leading powers had concluded with Tehran in 2015 to limit Iran's nuclear program. The EU has even developed plans to thwart Washington's reimposition of sanctions.[17] Those are encouraging signs of greater policy independence, but how deep or sustained that defiance will be in the coming months and years remains to be seen.

On other issues, the continuation of the traditional patron-dependent transatlantic relationship clearly has continued—and even escalated in some respects. That is especially true as concerns about possible Russian intimidation or aggression deepened in the past few years.

Some European members of NATO have become at least modestly more serious about addressing security concerns and boosting their tangible military capabilities. Others, including Europe's leading economic power, Germany, have not done so.

Nearly all of NATO's European members make securing a greater, even more reliable U.S. commitment to Europe's protection a higher priority than strengthening their own military capacities. The emphasis on getting Washington to increase the number and size of its force deployments in Eastern Europe demonstrates the relative priorities. Take, for example, the lobbying effort that Poland and other eastern members of NATO have conducted to induce the United States to establish permanent military bases in their countries. The underlying goal clearly is to make the U.S. tripwire larger and supposedly more credible.

The persistence of the de facto patron-client relationship is toxic for both sides, but especially so for the United States. Washington should recognize that it is unwise to insist on Europe being a perpetual security dependent, as though little has changed from the days of a weak and demoralized democratic Europe in the decade following the end of World War II. Today's Europe has significant security capabilities of its own and could easily make those capabilities even more robust if its leaders chose to do so. A new European-controlled security association would become a true ally, not a minimally helpful adjunct, if a major threat to the transatlantic community actually did arise—as opposed to the current hyped threat of a revanchist Russia.

Recognizing and encouraging greater European security initiatives, instead of discouraging, obstructing, and torpedoing them would benefit America's long-term interests. Washington could offload completely onto the major European powers the responsibility for managing subregional security problems, such as the simmering disputes in the Balkans. The United States could even commence reducing the U.S. security profile in the Middle East and transferring the bulk of responsibility for dealing with that troubled region to European powers who are much closer geographically and have far more interests at stake.

NATO's European members already have impressive strengths as measured in terms of both population size and economic power. With some additional efforts, including setting better priorities and developing more extensive multilateral intra-European defense cooperation and coordination, they could develop impressive military capabilities as well. The foundation for a more serious security role is already in place.

A Strong Economic Foundation for Building a Strong Military

Several of the European countries are elite economic powers. According to the World Bank, Germany has the world's fourth largest economy, behind only those of the United States, China, and Japan. Great Britain has the fifth largest; France, the seventh; and Italy, the ninth.[18] The most recent data from the International Monetary Fund put Germany's annual GDP at $4.21 trillion, Great Britain's at $2.94 trillion, and France's just behind at $2.93 trillion. Even Italy at $2.18 trillion and Spain at $1.51 trillion are serious economic players.[19] NATO Europe (the alliance membership minus the United States and Canada) has a collective GDP of more than $19 trillion. Compare that total to Russia's $1.6 trillion: NATO Europe has an economic output literally more than 10 times that of its principal potential adversary.

A significant disparity between the EU nations and Russia also exists in terms of military spending. Granted, the spending of NATO's European members remains far more modest than the huge U.S. defense budget, which is projected to reach $750 billion in 2019. Britain and France have defense budgets of $56.1 billion and $53.4 billion, respectively. Italy spends just $24.9 billion annually, and Germany, despite its status as the world's number four economic power, spends only $45.7 billion on defense.[20]

Still, the annual collective defense spending level of those leading European powers exceeds $180 billion. That figure significantly eclipses Russia's $63.1 billion.[21] Moreover, including the spending of the smaller members adds another $84 billion, meaning that NATO Europe outspends Russia by over a 4 to 1 margin. Moreover, as noted in Chapter 4, if the European nations consider Moscow a truly existential threat, they are fully capable of spending more—much more.

Even given their chronic parsimonious investments in defense, several of the European NATO countries can field militaries with significant conventional capabilities. Many of the newer members are mini-states with extremely small armed forces that would be of little use in a major conflict—especially one with Russia. Other members, though, have the ability to put up a credible resistance to an act of aggression. Turkey, for example, has 355,200 active duty military personnel with another 378,700 in reserve units, plus another 156,800 paramilitary personnel. The Turkish military is equipped with battle tanks, rocket launchers, attack helicopters, jet fighters, and sophisticated air defense batteries (ironically now including the Russian-supplied S-400).[22]

Germany, democratic Europe's natural economic and security leader, has unfortunately allowed its military to atrophy to a disturbing extent since the end of the Cold War, creating (among other problems) insufficient readiness levels and shortages of key spare parts. Nevertheless, Berlin's forces still would pose a barrier to any invader. Germany's active-duty military of 178,600 can deploy an array of modern weaponry, including Leopard battle tanks, AP-3C Orion anti-submarine aircraft, and 123 Eurofighter Typhoons.[23]

Before the bulk of an invasion force could even reach Germany, it would have to get through Poland. That task might not be all that easy. Although Warsaw only began a serious push to meet NATO's 2 percent GDP target for military spending after Russia's seizure of Crimea and support of separatism in eastern Ukraine in 2014, its spending has now reached that level. Polish leaders may be devoting considerable effort to securing a permanent U.S. military presence in their country, but they also are building up Poland's own military. Warsaw's 105,000 active-duty force is backed by 73,400 paramilitary fighters. As with Germany and several other NATO members, Polish ground forces deploy various models of the Leopard battle tank. In Poland's case, nearly 1,000 of those weapon systems are available. The air force jet fighters are more limited, but several dozen are available.[24] Polish defenders certainly could not defeat an invading force on their own, but they seem capable of slowing it down substantially.

The military capabilities on Germany's western flank are even more impressive, giving a European defense effort strategic depth. France's active-duty military numbers 202,700, augmented by 103,400 paramilitary forces. Land forces have available some 200 Leclerc battle tanks as well as dozens of front-line artillery pieces, rocket launchers, and other weapons. Air and naval forces are even more capable. In addition to an aircraft carrier, the *Charles de Gaulle*, France sports a small but significant navy with nearly a dozen modern destroyers. The French air force boasts Mirage 200 and Rafale fighters.[25]

Additional European countries, such as Italy, Spain, Romania, and others, could (and in the event of a continent-wide security crisis almost certainly would) throw their military weight into the balance as well. Likewise, even if Brexit proceeds and Britain actually exits the EU, London would hardly remain indifferent to a major act of aggression in Europe. Its conventional capabilities are both modern and sizable. The UK's 85,000 ground force might not add that much to the capabilities of its Continental neighbors, but its naval forces and more than 200 combat aircraft are another matter.[26]

The bottom line is that Russia (much less a smaller aggressor) would have to consider some serious difficulties and risks if it decided to launch a war of aggression—especially anything that went beyond Russia's immediate border regions. Even without the United States, the European nations would be capable of mounting a resistance that would not be easy to overcome. And if those countries improved their capabilities by increasing military spending and setting better priorities for that spending, they could mount a ferocious resistance. Any leader in the Kremlin would have to consider the risks and take into account prospects for success that are far from certain. That lack of certainty itself is a rather effective deterrent.

A key challenge for the European powers in building an even more credible collective defense effort distinct from NATO is to increase the efficiency of their military spending, as well as the overall size. That means focusing more on useful, cutting-edge weapons systems and reducing spending on obsolete systems and glorified jobs programs for young, otherwise unemployed citizens. Finally, NATO Europe urgently needs to better coordinate the strategies and capabilities of the various national military forces. The current degree of duplication and waste means that the overall military spending of NATO Europe (or alternatively, the EU in alliance with post-Brexit Britain) does not come close to producing the potential military capability that the current amount of spending should produce.

With sufficient effort on the part of the European governments, those problems and limitations can be overcome or at least greatly diminished. Even in their current state, the collective militaries of democratic Europe would be a serious opponent for a revanchist Russia, if that menace ever emerged. And the existing forces are more than capable of dealing with any lesser threats that might arise from other sources.

The Issue of Nuclear Deterrence

Proponents of continued NATO primacy and U.S. dominance of the alliance raise the objection that Russia has a vast nuclear arsenal to augment its conventional military forces. Only two European members of NATO, Britain and France, possess any nuclear weapons, and their arsenals are small compared with Moscow's extensive array. Advocates of extended deterrence insist that maintaining the U.S. nuclear umbrella over the NATO allies and the tripwire forces in Europe are crucial to deter Russia from attempting to use its advantage in nuclear weaponry to intimidate other nations on the Continent.[27]

That argument has some validity but less than it might appear on the surface. Nuclear weapons have far more utility for deterrence than for intimidation, much less war fighting.[28] If a war breaks out, then that nuclear arsenal has failed in its principal role. The British and French national nuclear arsenals undoubtedly are eclipsed by the size of the Russian arsenal, but they are far from trivial. France has 280 deployed warheads. The principal platform is the ballistic missile submarine *Le Triomphant*, and several aircraft, including 20 Rafale M F3s and 23 Mirage 2000Ns, also carry such weapons. Britain has an arsenal of 215 strategic warheads, 120 of which are deployed aboard the ballistic missile submarine *Vanguard*, with the remainder kept in reserve but ready to be deployed on various delivery systems, if a crisis develops.[29]

Strategic arsenals of that size are large enough to be credible deterrents. Although Russia clearly would prevail in a nuclear exchange, Kremlin leaders know that their country would suffer massive damage from such a conflict. Therefore, only the most reckless Russian leader would contemplate launching an attack on its smaller nuclear rivals. Moreover, for the first time, a serious debate is emerging in Germany about that country joining the global nuclear weapons club.[30] Although the option has met with strong public resistance, it can no longer be dismissed as a possible development. Even a modest German deterrent would add to the complications that the Kremlin would face if it contemplated aggression against major European powers. Members of American and European political and opinion elites should at least be receptive to the possibility of a nuclear-armed Germany instead of acting as though that would be the most horrifying development imaginable.[31] Germany is a stable, conservative, democratic country; it is not a candidate to launch wars of aggression.

A more serious caveat is that while the British and French (and possibly future German) nukes might be sufficient to deter a Russian attack directly on their countries, they wouldn't necessarily deter an attack on the nonnuclear NATO members such as Poland, the Czech Republic, or Romania, much less the even more exposed and vulnerable Baltic republics. Extended deterrence inevitably has less credibility than direct deterrence, and it is a valid concern to wonder if Britain and France would risk their countries to defend nonnuclear European partners. Of course, many of the same policymakers, scholars, and journalists who question the credibility of a British or French nuclear umbrella over the rest of NATO Europe seem to have no problem assuming that an extended deterrence commitment from an even more geographically distant United States is indisputably credible.

Even if there are credibility issues with the belief that current British and French national nuclear capabilities could prevent Russian bullying of NATO's easternmost members, London and Paris could decide to enlarge the size and sophistication of their nuclear forces. Germany and other economically and technologically capable European powers also could opt to join the ranks of nuclear weapons powers —even though deciding to terminate their memberships in the Nuclear Non-Proliferation Treaty would certainly entail substantial diplomatic costs.

Moreover, contrary to the conventional wisdom that nuclear proliferation is inherently destabilizing and that all forms of proliferation are equally bad, prominent foreign policy scholars—including John Mearsheimer, Christopher Layne, and the late Kenneth Waltz—have made strong arguments that proliferation, by raising the potential costs and other adverse consequences of initiating even small conventional wars among major powers, actually has stabilizing effects.[32] That thesis is expressed in colloquial terms as "an armed society is a polite society." As a variation on the proliferation of national arsenals, democratic Europe can make a decision to use the British and French arsenals as the core for establishing a new, multilaterally controlled deterrent to protect all of the member states.

None of those possibilities involves easy decisions, but the Europeans should have the responsibility to address the problems and options to move beyond the sterile policy of relying on the United States to preserve the security status quo. Such a reliance is especially unwise when conditions are eroding the credibility of the U.S. global extended deterrence guarantee by the day.

Signs of New, Independent European Security Initiatives

One, perhaps inadvertent, benefit of President Trump's periodic negative comments about NATO is that some European leaders are again considering more seriously Europeans-only security options. As early as August 2016 at a meeting of the Central European Visegrád countries, Hungary's prime minister, Viktor Orbán, proposed creating an independent European Union army. The Czech Republic's prime minister seconded that idea. Lower-level European political figures had floated that scheme previously from time to time, but it had not gone far, nor had such a prominent leader endorsed it.[33]

Not surprisingly, France seems to be taking the lead in promoting options for a more substantive and independent European security posture.

France has long been NATO's maverick member. That has been true since the days of President Charles de Gaulle, who both developed an independent nuclear deterrent despite Washington's complaints and pulled France out of the alliance's integrated military command. And as noted in Chapter 2, Paris initially pushed for alternatives to NATO being the exclusive security institution for post–Cold War Europe.

Now Washington's habitual insistence on NATO (U.S.) primacy is being tested again. President Emmanuel Macron has seized the initiative in the latest manifestation of greater European security assertiveness. In particular, he has made several proposals for a European Union military. Macron explicitly revived the idea for an independent EU army in the fall of 2017.[34] In a speech to French ambassadors in late August 2018, he expanded on his idea, stating that Europe needed to take more responsibility for its own defense and stop relying on the United States for its security. In a subsequent speech to an EU gathering later in the week, Macron called for a "nearly automatic" mutual security guarantee within the EU in light of Washington's apparent wavering commitment to international (including European) security.

Although he denied that such a scheme was designed to undermine or supersede NATO, Macron clearly sought a vigorous European military capability to operate outside of NATO. Macron contended that Europe had depended far too long on the United States for protection. "Our aim is clearly for Europe to achieve strategic autonomy and reinforce defence solidarity," he stated bluntly. Such a goal required only "minor changes" to the Lisbon Treaty (the EU's governing document), Macron insisted.[35]

Although France is taking the lead in proposing a substantially more independent European security policy and capability, it is hardly alone. In June 2018—just before the tense confrontation with Trump at the Brussels NATO summit—nine EU nations signed onto the French plan to establish a "Defense Intervention Group" to facilitate an independent military intervention in the event of aggression or disorder inside or outside EU territory. The measure also sought to facilitate continued defense cooperation between EU nations and Great Britain following that country's expected implementation of Brexit. Notably, Angela Merkel gave Germany's support for Macron's plan for such a European intervention force.[36]

Merkel has seemed nearly as uncertain as Macron about the continued reliability of the U.S. commitment to protect Europe. She stated that greater EU unity, a common foreign policy, and a more robust focus on security issues "is what we will need for our own survival because the nature of conflicts has changed completely since the end of the Cold War. A great many global conflicts are taking place on Europe's doorstep. And it is not the case that the United States of America will simply protect us. Instead, Europe must take its destiny in its own hands. That is our job for the future."[37]

Other European political figures are voicing similar, sometimes even more assertive, views about the need for a serious EU security role. "Only together, we are strong," Michael Gahler, a German member of the European Parliament, said in July 2018 after the approval of a €500 million fund for research and development of defense industrial products. "Only united will Europeans face the challenges that emanate from Russia, disintegrating states in the neighborhood and, unfortunately, the currently incalculable U.S. foreign and security policy."[38] In December 2017, the European Parliament endorsed the creation of a "directorate general for defense" to more effectively implement a common EU foreign policy and security policy.[39]

Such sentiments and expressed objectives could prove as hollow or stillborn as the proposed European Defense Community (EDC) in the 1950s or the previous push for the ESDP in the late 1990s and early 2000s. The idea of a European army dates back to the 1950s when French prime minister Rene Plevin first proposed the EDC. Under that plan, a European army would have responded to a defense minister who in turn responded to the EDC. The logic was that the capabilities of an integrated European defense were far greater than those of any one state individually. Collaborating countries would integrate their defense personnel and equipment into a European defense force, which would become a European military in a common uniform and recruited by common practices. A high commissioner for European defense would report to an EDC body made up of individual national defense ministers.

At the time of the EDC proposal, a key obstacle to an effective, integrated European defense was the task of agreeing to a division of labor and responsibility on a multilateral level. As long as EU members each insisted on maintaining national defense establishments with minimal multilateral coordination, except to some extent through NATO, establishing a credible Continental defense force was difficult. The reluctance to engage in the necessary intra-European defense sharing and collaboration was a key reason (along with resistance to West German rearmament) that the EDC plan failed.[40]

The same coordination problem has been a major factor in why subsequent proposals for a European army have similarly failed to launch. Given the daunting obstacles regarding a division of defense capabilities and responsibilities (along with the prospect of greater overall military spending), it simply has been easier for the European countries to continue to rely on NATO as the principal institutional mechanism for their defense—and rely on the United States as their ultimate security guarantor.

Nevertheless, dissatisfaction with the EU's military impotence has flared with greater frequency during the post–Cold War era. Tony Blair surprisingly abandoned the position that his predecessors had long adopted against autonomous European security initiatives and began working with French president Jacques Chirac to focus on a common EU defense outside of NATO. NATO's interventions in Bosnia and Kosovo during the 1990s also highlighted European defense deficiencies. The 60,000-man force would not—or could not—act as an EU standing army. Instead, units were pulled from national militaries on an ad hoc basis when necessary. The general inability to operate effectively with U.S. forces greatly troubled Blair.

His concerns were shared in other EU countries. But progress on rectifying those problems and establishing greater integrated capabilities was painfully slow. In May 2003, EU leaders came up with a European Capability Action Plan to attempt to close the gap between U.S. and European capabilities. Washington's NATO allies clearly had fallen far behind, and that realization was more than a little humiliating.

Given the long record of false starts and frustrations regarding the creation of an independent European defense capability, it is important to avoid getting carried away by recent moves toward that objective.

But there are subtle indications that those ambitions may be more substantive and enduring than previous episodes. For example, in June 2018, the European Commission proposed a €13 billion budget for a European Defense Fund. The stated justification was "to increase the EU's strategic autonomy, bolster the EU's ability to protect its citizens and make the EU a stronger global actor."[41] More European nations than ever before seem to be echoing the traditional French contention that Europe must operate in a more serious manner, and independent of the United States, than has been the case with earlier episodes.

It remains be seen, of course, whether an association of diverse countries actually can find the requisite unity to implement a common foreign policy, much less develop a unified EU military capable of operating as a cohesive, coordinated force. But worries about Washington's intentions and reliability are very real, and they are stimulating serious discussions about Europe's security role.

Entrenched defenders of the NATO status quo on either side of the Atlantic should not assume that nothing significant has changed or is likely to change. Signs are mounting of a new attitude about security issues and the role that Europe ought to play. Three experienced defense analysts detected a significant new element in the various moves regarding EU defense issues over the past year or so: "The mood in the European Union on military affairs is undergoing a seismic shift. Policymakers across the Continent finally agree that hard power—long viewed as antithetical to the EU's *raison d'être*—is now essential to the bloc's survival."[42] That shift is not trivial, and if it continues, it may have dramatic implications for the transatlantic security relationship and the future of NATO.

U.S. officials and their allies in the broader American foreign policy community show no increased receptivity toward the efforts of France and Germany to revive the European Union's security ambitions, though. John Bolton certainly has not altered his hostility to independent European security efforts over the years. He even repeated the "dagger aimed at NATO's heart" phrase in a September 17, 2016, op-ed in the *Boston Globe*—when he was angling for a high-level policy post if Republican presidential nominee Donald Trump won the upcoming election. "We can count on enthusiastic support from Britain and much of 'new Europe' for reforming and strengthening the alliance," Bolton wrote, "but when European governments place renewed emphasis on a purely European solution, we are seeing a dagger pointed at NATO's heart." He added, "If the EU, rather than its individual NATO member countries, really did develop a robust military capability, it would inevitably challenge the alliance's foundational concept."[43] When Bolton occupied an office in the West Wing just a few doors down from the Oval Office, he likely continued peddling that same animosity regarding independent European security initiatives to President Trump.

Washington needs to renounce its traditional antipathy to a strong European defense entity. Whether insisting on NATO primacy and U.S. hegemony made sense in the bipolar strategic environment of the Cold War is a moot point. Today's world is different in fundamental ways. Not only is democratic Europe much stronger and more capable of providing for its own defense, but not all security problems affect all portions of the West equally. To assume that disorders in the Balkans or elsewhere on Europe's periphery should be as important to the United States as to the EU countries is irrational. Such an assumption is no more logical than believing that the EU countries should be as concerned as the United States about the ongoing political struggle in Venezuela or possible problems in Central America or the Caribbean.[44]

Diverging Security Interests

As NATO increasingly pursued "out of area" missions during the 1990s and early 2000s, some NATO traditionalists in Europe became very uneasy about the implications for the Continent. Comments like those of Madeleine Albright, who suggested that NATO become a force for peace "from the Middle East to Central Africa," did not ease such apprehension.[45] Indeed, Albright's former Clinton administration colleagues Warren Christopher and William Perry urged the alliance to be an instrument for the projection of force anywhere the West's "collective interests" were threatened.[46]

French Foreign Minister Hubert Vedrine cautioned against that approach, warning that it ran the risk "of diluting the alliance."[47]

Without a reasonably tight geographic focus, NATO could become a global crusader, endangering European interests in remote arenas. Spanish Foreign Minister Abel Matutes was even more specific that Europe did not have a stake in every geopolitical problem the United States might want to address somewhere else in the world. He stressed that what happens "8,000 kilometers from us—in Korea, for example . . . cannot be considered a threat to our security." Vedrine echoed that point, saying that NATO "is the North Atlantic Treaty Organization, not the North Pacific."[48] Such comments indicated an explicit recognition that American and European interests were distinct and separable, not identical or even always compatible.

Charles Krauthammer, Henry Kissinger, and other opinion leaders who adopted a restrictive view of NATO's proper mission also made that important distinction from the American side two decades ago during the Kosovo crisis. Kissinger argued that "Kosovo is no more a threat to America than Haiti is to Europe—and we never asked for help there." He worried about blurring such important differences and having Washington deal with every manner of parochial problem in or near Europe. "Is NATO to be the home for a whole series of Balkan NATO protectorates?" Kissinger asked.[49]

The answer to his question was not clear at the time, but it is now. The United States is still entangled in the Balkans, trying to help resolve quarrels between Serbia and now-independent Kosovo. Washington even dispatched a 500-person troop contingent in 2017 to bolster the international peacekeeping force there when tensions flared sharply.[50] The U.S. government also is on the front lines of dealing with Russian-Ukrainian and Russian-Georgian disputes. U.S. leaders still have made no meaningful distinction between the interests of the United States and Europe.

That approach is illogical, excessively burdensome and needlessly dangerous. And recognition appears to be growing among populations in both Europe and the United States of diverging interests within the alliance. Public opinion surveys confirm that there are substantial and widening differences between American and European perspectives on a range of foreign policy issues.[51] That realization might well have taken root and grown after the first round of dissent about NATO's "new missions" surfaced in the late 1990s. The 9/11 attacks and the onset of the so-called war on terror temporarily reinforced a sense of transatlantic solidarity, thereby stifling debate and needed policy changes. But that effect is fading.

The interests of Europe and America overlap, but they are not congruent. Creating a capable European security organization to handle purely European contingencies makes sense for both sides. Developing such a capability also would transform Europe into a true ally instead of a glorified U.S. protectorate, which could prove crucial if it ever became necessary to confront a serious menace to the entire transatlantic community. Admittedly, that scenario appears to be unlikely, despite overblown concerns about Russia's intentions, but such a development can't be ruled out. U.S. leaders should encourage European ambitions for an independent security capability, not blindly follow previous administrations and seek to sabotage those ambitions. And the United States should insist that such an organization take primary responsibility for the Continent's security affairs.

CONCLUSION

TOWARD A FLEXIBLE, 21ST-CENTURY TRANSATLANTIC SECURITY RELATIONSHIP

It would seem self-evident that wise leaders should always seek to maintain the maximum degree of flexibility and choice in foreign policy. Commitments and strategies that may make sense under one set of conditions can become obsolete and even counterproductive when circumstances change. Therefore, locking one's country into a set of rigid, long-term obligations is imprudent and potentially very risky.

Unfortunately, NATO is the premier example of U.S. leaders' willingness—indeed eagerness—to violate that important principle. NATO was created to deal with the Cold War; it is not only obsolete for the conditions of the 21st century, it has become a dangerous albatross around the neck of the American republic. U.S. leaders continue going out of their way to limit America's policy options in order to "reassure" an expanding roster of European security dependents that the United States remains willing to incur any risk and pay any price to protect its alliance partners. That policy badly needs to change.

Rigid, obsolete commitments have caused problems for great powers throughout history. Perhaps the most tragic example occurred during the years leading up to World War I. Europe's major countries had divided themselves into rival security blocs, the Triple Entente and the Triple Alliance. When tensions soared in 1914 following the assassination of Archduke Franz Ferdinand, the heir to the Austro-Hungarian throne, those alliances transformed an emotional, but limited, dispute between Austria and tiny Serbia into a continental crisis.

Germany concluded that it must back its shaky, increasingly decrepit Austrian ally's attempt to coerce Belgrade. When the Russian Empire chose to protect its Serbian client, Germany responded with warnings to Moscow. France then felt pressured to back its Russian ally, and the die was cast for war between the Triple Entente and the Triple Alliance as rival military forces mobilized for action. The process illustrates Georgetown University professor Earl C. Ravenal's later trenchant observation that alliances are "transmission belts for war."[1] A bilateral, subregional quarrel became a monstrous global conflict that consumed millions of lives. Today's NATO is the potential incubator for a similar catastrophe.

The fear of being locked into unjustified and dangerous security commitments was a key reason why America's founders were so averse to "entangling alliances." In his Farewell Address, George Washington made an important distinction between permanent and temporary alliances.[2] He asserted that the United States should "steer clear of permanent alliances with any portion of the foreign world." Such obligations would tie the republic to partners for unforeseen contingencies far into the future. Conversely, Washington acknowledged that "we may safely trust to temporary alliances for extra-ordinary emergencies." The distinction was astute and in no way reflected the simplistic notion of "isolationism." Instead, the strategy embodied the principle of selectivity, and it expressed a shrewd note of caution that is even more relevant today than it was in Washington's time. NATO, in particular, has become the ultimate "permanent alliance," with all the defects and perils of such an arrangement.

Later influential American political figures echoed Washington's admonition to preserve the maximum degree of choice and flexibility in U.S. foreign policy. Both in his Senate speeches opposing ratification of the North Atlantic Treaty and in his subsequent book, *A Foreign Policy for Americans*, Sen. Robert A. Taft (R-OH) stressed those points. He dubbed his approach the policy of "the free hand."[3] That standard also should be the core principle of a new U.S. transatlantic security policy in the 21st century.

Overcoming Stale Thinking and Vested Interests

A more limited and flexible approach would not imply U.S. indifference to geostrategic developments in Europe. It certainly would not be based on the silly notions that knee-jerk advocates of the policy status quo always trot out—the canard that a more selective strategy amounts to "isolationism" or "turning our backs on the world" or renouncing all aspects of "U.S. leadership." We are long past the time to move the NATO policy debate beyond such overwrought, mind-numbing clichés and discuss meaningful policy choices.

Unfortunately, pro-NATO types cling ever more tenaciously to an outdated status quo. Indeed, many of them express a sneering resentment toward the mere suggestion that NATO has outlived its usefulness or that Americans should consider alternative policies.[4] An especially ugly (and increasingly frequent) allegation is that any proposals along those lines play into the hands of Vladimir Putin—and, at least in President Trump's case, are intended to do so. Retired Admiral James Stavridis, former supreme allied commander at NATO, made that argument explicitly. In a January 2019 *Time* article, he even asserted that a U.S. withdrawal from NATO would make "only Putin happy."[5]

Notably, passionate NATO defenders like Stavridis typically have had careers in which the alliance has played a central role. For such people, phasing out a U.S.-led NATO threatens their careers, institutional missions, and professional identities. The negative effect would be a wider version of the shocking impact on Soviet studies specialists when the USSR disintegrated. Not surprisingly, NATO careerists resist ferociously any prospect of such professional irrelevance.

The financial dimension to the campaign to preserve and expand NATO also is extensive. It was hardly a coincidence that one of the top leaders of the U.S. Committee on NATO—the principal lobby for enlarging the alliance in the late 1990s—was Bruce L. Jackson, who happened to be vice president of Lockheed. That company and other defense firms benefited handsomely when NATO added Central and East European nations to the alliance.[6] The new members became eligible to purchase state-of-the-art weapons systems to upgrade their defense forces, and U.S. officials promptly prodded them to take such steps so that their militaries would become fully compatible with the alliance's defense strategy and capabilities.

The financial stakes involved in retaining and expanding NATO as the leading component of Washington's security strategy are not confined to defense firms, however. An array of think tanks, university departments, and consulting firms would find their roles diminished—perhaps greatly diminished—if the United States left the alliance and adopted a more limited, selective posture toward Europe. It is striking that much of the shrill opposition to any change in America's NATO policy comes from entities such as the Atlantic Council and the Marshall Fund, which enjoy generous funding from not only U.S. defense-related firms but European governments and their thinly disguised front organizations as well.

Finally, some of the biggest beneficiaries of a continued dominant U.S. role in transatlantic security affairs are the Pentagon and intelligence agencies. Justifying a $750 billion annual military budget (which the White House has proposed for fiscal year 2020) would be extremely difficult if the United States adopted a more limited posture regarding Europe—especially if that new policy also entailed a major reduction in Washington's Middle East involvement. An enhanced focus on East Asia (especially China) might offset such changes to some extent, but shrinkage in budgets, personnel levels, and career opportunities would be inevitable. And the prospect of such changes would be deeply threatening to an array of entrenched interests throughout those bureaucracies.

None of that means there is a vast organized conspiracy to discredit NATO critics and do whatever is necessary to preserve and enhance NATO. But the various incentives do foster group think and a herd mentality in favor of the alliance. Such a phenomenon is unhealthy for any policy debate, but it is especially so regarding the future of U.S. security policy toward Europe. Continuing the blunders that have marked Washington's European policies since the demise of the Soviet Union is not only wasteful but increasingly perilous. Rote invocations of the alleged need for an endless U.S. commitment to NATO do not change that reality.

Despite the obstacles, we must overcome the stifling influence of stale thinking and vested interests regarding NATO. Article 5 is a de facto automatic commitment to go to war if an ally (however trivial or strategically irrelevant) becomes embroiled in an armed conflict, and such an obligation is more imprudent than ever before. The costs and risks of Washington's security obligations to European allies now substantially outweigh any existing or potential benefits. When a great power reaches that point with regard to any policy, the need for drastic change becomes imperative. America's NATO commitment has arrived at that point. U.S. leaders must craft a more nuanced and selective security relationship between the United States and Europe.

A fresh strategy would embody several important principles. The outcome of the debate about those principles may well determine whether the United States enjoys a prolonged era of peace or finds itself repeatedly drawn into conflicts that have little or no relevance to the fundamental interests of the American republic. Even more important, embracing the correct principles may determine whether the United States can avoid a cataclysmic military collision with Russia.

Distinguishing between Essential and Nonessential European Developments

A worthwhile new security strategy would recognize that although the United States has some important interests in Europe, not everything that occurs on the Continent is essential to America's well-being, much less to its survival as a secure, independent democratic society. The difference is vast between preventing a hostile would-be global hegemon from gaining control of Europe and trying to resolve every incident of political upheaval or every dispute among European nations. Most incidents, however disagreeable or disorderly, do not pose a potential existential (or even meaningful) threat to the United States.

The turmoil that accompanied the break-up of Yugoslavia in the 1990s is a prime example of a development that warranted no more than a minimal, purely diplomatic, U.S. effort. It certainly did not require America's military involvement, much less the assumption of the leadership role to micromanage the distribution of political power within the former Yugoslavia's successor states.

In addition to excessive involvement in a subregional conflict, Washington's Balkan policy was marked by inconsistency and double standards bordering on incoherence. U.S. leaders were tolerant and understanding about the cascade of secessions—except for such ambitions on the part of the Serbs. Clinton administration policymakers could never articulate a reason for tolerating—and even fostering—various separatist movements but insisting simultaneously that Serbs in newly minted independent Bosnia must be prevented from seceding and forming their own state. Moreover, the ultimate effect of Washington's micromanagement was to help establish and perpetuate two dysfunctional political entities, Bosnia and Kosovo, which then required ongoing (and apparently eternal) international aid and supervision.

A well-conceived strategy would have avoided such pitfalls. It would have realized that sorting out post-communist political arrangements in the Balkans did not constitute a systemic crisis that could create chaos throughout Europe and arguably impinge on crucial American interests. The nature, severity, or scale of the turbulence (much less all three factors combined) never came close to reaching the point that the United States needed to intervene. The events that did occur were modest, subregional changes that the major European powers, either through the European Union or on an ad hoc basis, could have—and should have—managed on their own. U.S. involvement, especially military involvement, should be reserved for negative developments that pose a serious problem for the entire transatlantic region, not merely a parochial conflict, however unfortunate, in a strategic backwater like the Balkans.

The counterargument that Balkan events triggered World War I does not alter the current reality. The geopolitical map and the power alignments it reflects is vastly different today from what it was in 1914.

Squabbles in the Balkans have little potential to trigger a great power war—unless Russia and the United States foolishly link their fortunes to rival Balkan clients. Obsessing about past eras is a key symptom of a foreign policy based on nostalgia, which is perhaps the principal underlying defect in current NATO policy. America's policy needs to look forward, not back.

What would constitute a European development that warranted a decision by Washington to intervene and take decisive action? If a global power and would-be European hegemon like Nazi Germany or the Soviet Union arose and began to make moves that indicated an extensive expansionist agenda, that development would clearly be a worry for the United States. Few Americans would be willing to tolerate the emergence of a hostile power capable of dominating Europe and intent on that goal. Washington's assistance to the Allied powers during an undeclared naval war against Germany in 1940 and 1941 (before the Japanese attack on Pearl Harbor brought the United States formally into World War II) reflected that unwillingness. So too did the four-decades-long containment policy against the USSR. Indeed, U.S. concern about the potential threat that a European hegemon might pose to the republic was evident long before the awful conflicts of the 20th century. Even Thomas Jefferson, who normally opposed U.S. entanglement in Europe's quarrels, was uneasy about a possible threat from Napoleonic France, given the extent of Napoleon's military triumphs.

In the unlikely event that a European security entity could not contain the rise of another hostile hegemonic power on the Continent, the United States might well have to intervene. But in the world of the 21st century, that scenario is exceedingly remote. NATO partisans are inclined to hype much more limited problems in an effort to preserve their cherished institution (and their own prominence), but such an approach is contrary to a prudent, sensible U.S. transatlantic policy appropriate for 21st-century realities. Americans should not allow such hyped fears to be a pretext for preserving an obsolete policy that perpetuates Washington's attempted micromanagement of Europe's security affairs.

Accepting and Encouraging an Independent Europe

Another badly needed feature of a new transatlantic policy for the United States is a willingness to treat the European Union (or even an alliance limited to the handful of major European powers) as a credible security actor, not a perpetual U.S. dependent or obedient junior partner. European military capabilities are far from trivial, although they can and probably should be enhanced. Most security problems that have arisen on Europe's perimeter are not major threats that bring important American interests into play. The roster of more modest problems includes the mundane territorial disputes between Russia and its neighbors, Georgia and Ukraine.

As in the case of instability in the Balkans, such developments are far more relevant to the European nations than they are to the United States. Europe's principal powers not only *can* handle those challenges on their own, they should be expected to do so. Insisting that all security issues be addressed and resolved through NATO—with Washington in charge of policy—is a manifestation of obsolete thinking that imposes needless burdens and responsibilities onto the United States. It is a strategy based on national narcissism.

Not only should the major European powers, through either the EU or another Europeans-only mechanism, be in charge of dealing with all mundane disruptions on the Continent itself, they should have responsibility for addressing adverse developments in the Middle East and North Africa (the Greater Middle East). That region is adjacent to Europe but thousands of miles from America. For Washington to take charge of efforts to preserve stability, protect the oil flow, prevent human rights abuses, and confront the multitude of other problems that bedevil that chronically volatile part of the world is unfair and unrealistic. Events in the Greater Middle East clearly have a direct impact to varying degrees on the well-being of European countries. The wave of refugees fleeing war-torn Middle East nations and causing political, economic, and social strains throughout Europe is an example of the region's substantial relevance to the Continent.

The impact of unpleasant Greater Middle East developments on the United States is far milder by virtue of greater distance. America's minimal dependence on oil from that area also gives this country more options than those available to European powers. Moreover, Washington's track record in trying to manage Greater Middle East affairs to maintain stability there is dismal. Even before the recent U.S.-created fiascos in Iraq, Libya, and Syria, America's meddling in the Middle East created far more problems than it solved. A half-century of Washington's geostrategic bungling in the Middle East was a major contributing factor to the rise of anti-U.S. terrorism, culminating in the 9/11 attacks, an especially graphic manifestation of blowback from Washington's clumsy, tone-deaf behavior. Similarly, the current refugee crisis—and the domestic political fissures it has created or worsened in numerous European nations—is largely the result of unwise geopolitical initiatives that the United States has pursued, often dragging its NATO allies along for the ride.

Given their own history of colonial misdeeds in the 19th and early 20th centuries (especially by Britain and France), the European powers would confront significant obstacles of their own to developing a united, coherent policy regarding the turbulent Greater Middle East. But they could scarcely do worse than the U.S. record in recent decades. Because they have more at stake than does America with respect to Middle East affairs, they should have responsibility for policy toward their difficult neighbors. American involvement, to the extent that it takes place at all, should be confined to a marginal, supportive role.

Recognizing that Spheres of Influence Remain a Geopolitical Reality

The most plausible case for preserving a dominant U.S. role in transatlantic security affairs through NATO is that it would be an insurance policy against the reemergence of a rogue great power that could pose a pervasive security menace. U.S. leaders and those in some European members of NATO clearly have designated Russia for that role already. But their view is based on either misperceptions or a deliberate attempt to create a new rationale for preserving and strengthening NATO.

Whatever the motive, the strategy is both dangerous and unnecessary. A willingness on the part of the Western powers to accept a modest Russian sphere of influence and treat that country's government with a modicum of respect would solve most of the current problems in East-West relations and greatly reduce tensions. Adopting a less confrontational course, however, requires more realistic thinking on the part of U.S. and European policymakers. In particular, it means recognizing that spheres of influence are still very much a part of the international system and that major powers are likely to insist on enjoying that prerogative. Indeed, Russia is hardly the only power to do so.

Unfortunately, too many U.S. officials seemingly regard the idea that major powers will insist on maintaining spheres of influence distasteful and illegitimate. Both Condoleezza Rice, George W. Bush's second secretary of state, and John Kerry, Barack Obama's second secretary of state, made that argument explicitly. They were adamantly unwilling to acknowledge that Russia could have such a zone of preeminence.[7] Indeed, Rice condemned the entire concept for any country as "archaic."[8]

Adopting a more realistic, nuanced position regarding spheres of influence would require modifying the professed faith of U.S. officialdom that the United States is the leader—and has been since the end of World War II—of a liberal, "rules-based" international order. Under that system, all countries are supposed to abide by the strictures of international law. Among those strictures is the insistence that a country not threaten, intimidate, or bully other countries—much less use military force to seize territory.

The history of the post–World War II era, however, confirms that the United States and its allies have violated those principles whenever it seemed convenient to do so.[9] It is very hard to square a liberal, rules-based international system with episodes such as the U.S.-led military interventions in Vietnam and Iraq, NATO's military missions in the Balkans, the NATO-assisted overthrow of Libya's Muammar Qaddafi, or the ongoing military meddling by the United States and several allies in Syria. The same point is true about sleazy covert actions that the CIA and allied intelligence agencies have undertaken, including military coups in such places as Iran and Guatemala during the Cold War. Finally, U.S. officials have shown no qualms about shielding allied countries when those allies commit blatant violations of international norms, even when violations include brazen land grabs or the commission of war crimes. Thus, Washington has remained content with Turkey's seizure of northern Cyprus, Israel's acquisition of the West Bank and annexation of the Golan Heights, and Saudi Arabia's atrocity-ridden war of aggression against Yemen. Indeed, both the Obama and Trump administrations actively assisted the Saudi war effort.[10]

Respecting the traditional concept of spheres of influence would require a reduced application of the power prerogatives that the United States has exercised since the end of World War II and intends to continue exercising. U.S. leaders implicitly assert the right to intervene anywhere in the world to advance America's foreign policy objectives. In practice, recent generations of policymakers have globalized the Monroe Doctrine; to them, America's rightful sphere of influence is "the sphere"—planet Earth.

But Russia and other major powers are not willing to accord the United States the status of global hegemon. They are digging in their heels and insisting that Washington respect their own (much more modest) spheres of influence. For Russia, that means asserting preeminence with respect to nations along its borders in both Eastern Europe and Central Asia. Moscow's position already is obvious regarding Georgia and Ukraine; a more subtle version is apparent in the Kremlin's dealings with the Central Asian republics.

Russia is not alone in pushing back against Washington's attempts at asserting global hegemony. China's behavior in the South China Sea and the Taiwan Strait provide ample indications that Beijing is setting limits to what it will tolerate from the United States.[11] The potential for miscalculations and unpleasant consequences in that part of the world are at least as great as they are in Europe between NATO and Russia.

To prevent the escalation of dangerous tensions with Moscow (and Beijing), U.S. leaders must dial back their insistence that all nations, even great powers, must adhere to the principles of a U.S.-led liberal, rules-based, international order. That system has been more fictional, or at least aspirational, than factual in any case. To maintain peace, American policymakers must accept that Russia and other great powers will insist upon and act according to the reality of spheres of influence. The objective of the EU powers, with Washington's quiet, limited support, should be to place some limits on the extent of the Russian sphere of influence, since at some point, Russia's concept will impinge on significant EU interests. The mission of effective diplomacy is to sort out such matters and set workable, recognizable limits on the ambitions of contending parties. But seeking to delegitimize the entire concept of spheres of influence is a nonstarter for even reasonably cordial East-West relations.

Worse is the apparent U.S. attitude that Russia is not entitled to even a minimal security zone adjacent to its homeland. Pushing to bring Ukraine and Georgia into NATO, after already incorporating the Baltic republics, reduces any Russian security buffer to a nullity. Conducting NATO military exercises within mere miles (and in at least one case, barely hundreds of yards) of the Russian border highlights such menacing arrogance. A fundamental change in Washington's approach is essential.

A Prudent, Sustainable 21st-Century Transatlantic Security Policy

The basic principles of an improved transatlantic security relationship are reasonably easy to discern. One key component recognizes that while American and European security interests overlap, they also diverge in many cases. It also requires a more flexible security structure so that the United States does not intervene in every unpleasant development that Europe might encounter. Only when vital interests on both sides of the Atlantic are at stake is joint action warranted. Less severe and more geographically limited problems in Europe can and should be addressed by regional or even subregional actors.

A second component acknowledges that the European Union already is a leading global economic player, and that the European nations acting either through that body or another Europeans-only mechanism should play a security role commensurate with that economic power. In particular, the United States needs to accept democratic Europe as a capable, independent geostrategic player, not an American junior partner at best and security protectorate at worst. Accepting that change in the transatlantic power structure means understanding how much the world has changed since the United States put a weak, devastated Europe behind the American security shield seven decades ago. Instead of attempting to obstruct that change, U.S. leaders should encourage Europe to become a robust, independent actor in world affairs. Although that change would reduce Washington's preeminent status and even dilute its influence, the potential rewards, especially the long-term rewards, greatly outweigh such losses.

A third component of a more enlightened, effective policy recognizes that Russia, for all its flaws, is not a messianic expansionist power. Treating Russia as merely a more recent incarnation of the Soviet Union has been counterproductive, if not corrosive, to prospects for regional and global peace. Moscow does not pose an existential threat either to the United States or to Europe. Russia may behave from time to time as a somewhat boorish—even overbearing—power, and that posture can make some of its neighbors uncomfortable. But Moscow's conduct is not out of the ordinary in how major regional powers tend to treat smaller, weaker neighbors. Such pressure is far more limited both in intensity and scope than the kind of threat that such countries as Napoleonic France, Nazi Germany, or the USSR posed. It is imperative that both the other European powers and the United States comprehend that crucial difference. A robust, engaged European security entity is quite capable of balancing a relatively mundane, if somewhat prickly, regional power like Russia. The United States should let such balancing behavior take its normal course.

The fourth component steps away from an exaggerated, inconsistent, and largely aspirational liberal international order as the operational reality in global or even European affairs. Longstanding features of international politics still apply, despite Western rhetoric to the contrary. Such features as security zones and spheres of influence are key aspects of international relations, however much some policymakers wish to deny that reality. A new, more effective transatlantic security strategy must acknowledge and respect a reasonable Russian sphere of influence on its perimeter, including in Eastern Europe. This policy would be based on both realism and restraint.

Abandoning the vain quest for U.S. global primacy includes no longer attempting to dominate Europe's security affairs. The United States is badly overextended militarily, politically, and economically. Embracing a more limited, selective role focusing on a reduced roster of policy goals has become urgent. One of the most feasible places to offload excessive responsibilities is Europe, which means it should also be one of the first. To do that, American leaders should propose a new relationship with an independent European security organization.

A Post-NATO Transatlantic Security Relationship

Transforming the European Union into an organization with security as well as economic responsibilities and powers would not be without its difficulties. Establishing a workable decisionmaking system involves a variety of challenges. One is whether consensus would be required, as is theoretically the case in NATO. (The reality is that Washington largely prevails on all issues that it regards as crucial; no other member has seemed strong enough or determined enough to engage in outright defiance in such cases, and Washington has shown a willingness to use brass-knuckles tactics, if necessary, to ensure that such a challenge does not take place.)

Since no member of the EU is powerful enough to exercise U.S.-style dominance in decisionmaking, consensus on security matters might have to be real, not just theoretical. As an alternative, EU members could collectively authorize the largest, most significant players to make the necessary security decisions, as long as those players are fully in accord. Whether within the EU or in a new security organization, the Europeans themselves would need to work out the specifics of a workable decisionmaking process.

In the absence of a purely European security body, NATO will likely soon face some of the same decisionmaking dilemmas, however. The growing discontent of France, Turkey, and Germany (among others) with Washington's domination of the alliance and questionable policy preferences indicates that the days of the United States exercising de facto control over all major decisions may be coming to an end.

Another problem that a Europeans-only security organization would have to resolve is whether to require members to maintain certain standards of human rights and democratic governance. Since Turkey is not an EU member, the rest of the EU would not necessarily have to decide whether to exclude that country. But what about the accelerating authoritarian trends in such existing members as Hungary and Poland? The overall membership of the European Union would have to decide whether or not rigorous political standards would be required for participation in a European defense alliance, or whether common security interests would be sufficient.

Trying to maintain the status quo of NATO primacy does not make resolving such problems much easier. The alliance still will have to confront the question of whether NATO is purely a security association or a league of democracies that insists upon certain internal political standards of all members. The growing demands in the United States and some other member states to discipline or even expel Turkey for the Erdoğan government's rogue behavior confirm that intra-NATO dilemma.

Similarly, questions about how to deal with Russia and how to address Middle East troubles are just two of the issues that will bedevil either NATO or a new European security institution. Indeed, the widening fissures between the United States and some of its leading NATO partners on both issues are harbingers of trouble. Trying to overcome such policy differences through NATO rather than the EU or a new European-controlled alliance may prove even more difficult and contentious, especially if American and European interests and policy priorities continue to diverge. Simply repeating mantras at every NATO conclave about enduring transatlantic solidarity is not a solution.

The European powers must address security challenges on their own and learn to live with the results. It does not help for the United States to encourage, if not insist upon, continued European dependence on U.S. protection—and continued deference to Washington's dominance. That approach merely retards the needed steps toward greater European policy independence and responsibility. Washington should encourage that maturation, not seek to obstruct it.

A Path Forward

Washington ought to adopt a strategy based on an orderly but prompt transfer of responsibility for Europe's security to the nations of democratic Europe. The Trump administration should give notice that the

United States intends to withdraw from the North Atlantic Treaty in April 2024, the 75th anniversary of the treaty. It is important not to extend the withdrawal process beyond such a deadline. A longer time frame would merely tempt many of the European allies to spend the first several years lobbying the United States to reverse its decision. The 2024 deadline still gives the allies sufficient time to forge a credible defense and foreign policy successor—if they move promptly to adjust to the new reality.

In addition to the comprehensive policy shift, U.S. leaders must commence a withdrawal of U.S. forces from the European theater. The United States ought to complete the withdrawal of all ground units within two years. It also should reduce its naval and air forces in Europe by at least 50 percent by that same date, with the goal of ending a permanent presence of such forces on the treaty's termination. The option of occasional deployments of U.S. air and naval units should be kept open, depending on the specifics of agreements with the responsible European security organization and Washington's own assessment of the overall security environment. Care must be taken, though, that such periodic, limited deployments do not become perpetual, large-scale "rotational" deployments that amount to a permanent U.S. military presence in all but name.

Unfortunately, the desperation of NATO partisans to preserve their institution seems to know no bounds. The House of Representatives' passage of the NATO Support Act in January 2019, barring the use of funds to facilitate U.S. withdrawal from the alliance in any way, is symptomatic of that attitude.[12] The constitutionality of such legislation is highly suspect. Presidents have enjoyed wide latitude regarding both troop deployments and continued adherence to treaties throughout America's history. A transparent congressional attempt to usurp that authority and seek to micromanage U.S. foreign policy warrants a challenge in the courts if necessary. Whoever occupies the White House over the next five years should—and certainly should have the legal latitude to—implement needed policy changes regarding NATO.

Great wailing and despair from the NATO preservation crowd on both sides of the Atlantic will inevitably accompany any meaningful policy shift. But 75 years is an exceedingly long period for any policy to be relevant and beneficial (much less optimal), and America's NATO membership is no exception. Indeed, it seems to epitomize the problem of policy entropy. A U.S.-led NATO is now well beyond its appropriate expiration date. It is time to accord the alliance the retirement celebration that should have been held when the Cold War came to an end and the Soviet Union dissolved.

Moving to a new, more restrained posture does not mean that the United States will take no interest in Europe's affairs. We need to reject the simplistic "light switch model" of America's engagement in the world, with only two possible settings: "off or on."[13] There are many settings between those two extremes, and there are multiple forms of engagement—diplomatic, economic, and cultural, as well as security.

Every effort should be made to preserve a robust, mutually beneficial transatlantic economic relationship. The United States also can and should maintain extensive diplomatic and cultural connections with Europe. And Washington should establish a consultative body either with a new European security organization or with the Continent's main military powers to address issues of mutual concern. Beyond that aspect, there is nothing to prevent joint military exercises and even temporary deployments of U.S. air and naval units, if the security environment turns more threatening. The point is just that America should not seek to be Europe's permanent security blanket and hegemon.

This more flexible approach would constitute an updated version of Robert A. Taft's policy of the free hand. Moreover, it would be one component of a U.S. global grand strategy based on realism and restraint.[14] America would no longer shackle itself to commitments that have more drawbacks than benefits or those that lock the republic into obligations that no longer make sense. It would end the thankless, unproductive strategy of trying to micromanage the security affairs of both Europe and the neighboring Middle East. For U.S. leaders to seek to deny their own country the essential element of policy choice is perverse. Indeed, a sustainable transatlantic policy for the 21st century must rest firmly on the principle of maximum choice for the United States.

NOTES

Introduction

1. Ryan Teague Beckwith, "Read Donald Trump's 'America's First' Foreign Policy Speech," *Time*, April 27, 2016. Emphasis added.

2. Gregg Zoroya, "Trump's Pay-or-Else NATO Comments Send a Chill through Europe," *USA Today*, July 21, 2016.

3. Quoted in Joe Gould, "World Reacts to Trump's Apparent Conditional Support for NATO Allies," *Defense News*, July 21, 2016.

4. Quoted in Krishnadev Calamur, "NATO Shmato?" *The Atlantic*, July 21, 2016.

5. Veronica Stracqualursi and Jim Acosta, "New York Times: Trump Raised Withdrawing the U.S. from NATO Several Times during 2018," CNN.com, January 16, 2019.

6. Joe Gould, "Trump Says U.S. Backs NATO '100%,' after Report He Discussed Withdrawal," *Defense News*, January 17, 2019.

7. Thomas Wright, "Trump's NATO Article 5 Problem," *Order from Chaos* (blog), Brookings Institution, May 17, 2017.

8. Rosie Gray, "Trump Declines to Affirm NATO's Article 5," *The Atlantic*, May 25, 2017.

9. Robbie Gramer, "Trump Discovers Article 5 after Disastrous NATO Visit," *Foreign Policy*, June 9, 2017.

10. Zachary Cohen, Michelle Kosinski, and Barbara Starr, "Trump's Barrage of Attacks 'beyond Belief,' Reeling NATO Diplomats Say," CNN Politics, July 12, 2018.

11. National Security Council policy document NSA 82. See U.S. Department of State, Office of the Historian, *Foreign Relations of the United States, 1950, Western Europe*, Vol. III, ed. David H. Stauffer et al. (Washington, Government Printing Office, 1977), https://history.state.gov/historicaldocuments/frus1950v03.

12. James McAllister, *No Exit: America and the German Problem, 1943–1954* (Ithaca, NY: Cornell University Press, 2001), p. 18.

13. Quoted in "Dulles Formulated and Conducted U.S. Foreign Policy for Six Decades," *On This Day: Obituary, New York Times*, May 25, 1959.

14. Alan Tonelson, "NATO Burden-Sharing: Promises, Promises," in *NATO Enters the 21st Century*, ed. Ted Galen Carpenter (London: Frank Cass Publishers, 2001), p. 38.

15. Christopher Layne, *The Peace of Illusions: American Grand Strategy from 1940 to the Present* (Ithaca, NY: Cornell University Press, 2006).

16. U.S. Department of State, Office of the Historian, *Foreign Relations of the United States, 1961–1963*, Vol. VIII, *National Security Policy*, ed. David W. Mabon (Washington: Government Printing Office, 1996), https://history.state.gov/historicaldocuments/frus1961-63v08.

17. For an updated, well-articulated version of the kind of U.S. strategy that the European allies feared (and continue to fear), see Elbridge Colby, "America Must Prepare for 'Limited War,'" *National Interest* (Online), October 21, 2015.

18. Robert D. McFadden, "Harold Brown, Defense Secretary in Carter Administration, Dies at 91," *New York Times*, January 5, 2019.

19. Michael Birnbaum, "Gates Rebukes European Allies in Farewell Speech," *Washington Post*, June 10, 2011.

20. Jim Garamone, "Hagel Urges European NATO Members to Boost Defense Budgets," American Forces Press Service, *DoD News*, June 4, 2014.

21. White House, "Remarks by the Vice President at the Munich Security Conference," February 18, 2017.

22. U.S. Department of Defense, "Remarks by Secretary Mattis at the Munich Security Conference in Munich, Germany," February 17, 2017.

23. Niall McCarthy, "Defense Expenditures of NATO Members Visualized [Infographic]," *Forbes*, July 10, 2018.

24. See Ted Galen Carpenter, *Gullible Superpower: U.S. Support for Bogus Foreign Democratic Movements* (Washington: Cato Institute, 2019), pp. 207–12; Josh Cohen, "Commentary: Ukraine's Neo-Nazi Problem," Reuters, March 19, 2018; and Stephen F. Cohen, "America's Collusion with Neo-Nazis," *The Nation*, May 2, 2018.

25. Alexander Clapp, "The Maidan Irregulars," *National Interest*, no. 143 (May-June 2016): 26–33.

26. Ted Galen Carpenter, "Ukraine Doesn't Deserve America's Blind Support," *American Conservative*, November 29, 2018, https://www.cato.org/publications/commentary/ukraine-doesnt-deserve-americas-blind-support.

27. Claudia Grisales, "House Lawmakers Approve New NATO Protections," *Stars and Stripes*, January 22, 2019.

28. Doug Bandow, "Today's NATO Mission Is to Preserve Itself," *American Conservative*, January 24, 2019, https://www.cato.org/publications/commentary/todays-nato-mission-preserve-itself.

Chapter One

1. David Owen, ed., *Bosnia-Herzegovina: The Vance-Owen Peace Plan* (Liverpool, UK: Liverpool University Press, 2013).

2. Charles Krauthammer, "By Rejecting Vance-Owen Plan, U.S. Now Responsible for Peace," *Deseret News*, February 14, 1993.

3. Quoted in Thomas L. Friedman, "Strains among Allies," *New York Times*, May 30, 1992, https://www.nytimes.com/1992/05/30/world/strain-among-allies.html.

4. Richard Holbrooke, *To End a War* (New York: Random House, 1998).

5. David Chandler, *Bosnia: Faking Democracy after Dayton,* 2nd ed. (London: Pluto Press, 2000).

6. Slobodan Lekic, "Ethnic Tensions Escalating in Bosnia, Where U.S. Troops Once Kept the Peace," *Stars and Stripes*, January 14, 2017; European Parliament, *2016 Commission Report on Bosnia and Herzegovina*, A8-0026/2017, February 6, 2017; and Andy Eckhardt and Vladimir Banic, "Bosnian War, 25 Years Later: Mostar Bridge Illustrates Lingering Divide," NBC News, March 19, 2017.

7. Christina Lamb, "Fear Returns to Bosnia as Putin Stirs Ethnic Tension," *The Times* (UK), April 1, 2018.

8. "Bosnia and Herzegovina Unemployment Rate," TradingEconomics.com, 2017–2018. The unemployment rate declined further to 34.48 percent in January 2019. Nevertheless, the rate averaged more than 42 percent over the period 2007 to 2019—an astonishingly high level. See "Bosnia and Hezegovina Unemployment Rate," TradingEconomics.com, 2018–2019, https://tradingeconomics.com/bosnia-and-herzegovina/unemployment-rate.

9. See James George Jatras, "NATO's Myths and Bogus Justifications for War," in *NATO's Empty Victory: A Postmortem on the Balkan War*, ed. Ted Galen Carpenter (Washington: Cato Institute, 2000), pp. 21–30; Doug Bandow, "NATO's Hypocritical Humanitarianism," in *NATO's Empty Victory*, ed. Carpenter, pp. 31–40; George Kenney, "Kosovo: On Ends and Means," *Nation*, December 27, 1999; and David Chandler, *From Kosovo to Kabul: Human Rights and International Intervention* (London: Pluto Press, 2002), pp. 73–75, 185.

10. Charles Krauthammer, "Floundering in Vainglory," *Washington Post*, April 16, 1999.

11. Ted Galen Carpenter and Malou Innocent, *Perilous Partners: The Benefits and Pitfalls of America's Alliances with Authoritarian Regimes* (Washington: Cato Institute, 2015), pp. 303–19.

12. Ted Galen Carpenter, "Moving beyond Self-Serving Myths: Acknowledging the Principal Cause of Radical Islamic Terrorism," *Cato@Liberty* (blog), December 14, 2015, https://www.cato.org/blog/moving-beyond-self-serving-myths-acknowledging-principal-cause-radical-islamic-terrorism.

13. Hillary Clinton, *Hard Choices* (New York: Simon and Schuster, 2014), p. 364.

14. Clinton, *Hard Choices*, p. 367.

15. Clinton, *Hard Choices*, p. 368.

16. Clinton, *Hard Choices*, p. 368.

17. Robert M. Gates, *Duty: Memoirs of a Secretary at War* (New York: Alfred A. Knopf, 2014), p. 518.

18. Clinton, *Hard Choices*, p. 370.

19. Clinton, *Hard Choices*, p. 371.

20. Gates, *Duty*, p. 516.

21. Clinton, *Hard Choices*, p. 374.

22. Clinton, *Hard Choices*, pp. 374–75.

23. Gates, *Duty*, p. 522.

24. Gates, *Duty*, pp. 511, 518.

25. Gates, *Duty*, p. 519.

26. Ted Galen Carpenter, *Gullible Superpower: U.S. Support for Bogus Foreign Democratic Movements* (Washington: Cato Institute, 2019), pp.173–87.

27. Clinton, *Hard Choices*, p. 377.

28. Gates, *Duty*, p. 515.

29. Ted Galen Carpenter, "The Populist Surge and the Rebirth of Foreign Policy Nationalism," *SAIS Review of International Affairs* 37, no.1 (Winter-Spring 2017): 33–46.

30. Steven A. Cook, "Emperor Erdoğan," *Politico*, February 3, 2015.

31. Harry Cockburn, "Turkey Coup: 2,700 Judges Removed from Duty Following Failed Overthrow Attempt," *The Independent* (UK), July 16, 2016.

32. "Licenses of 21,000 Turkish Teachers Have Been Revoked: Ministry Official," Reuters, July 19, 2016.

33. Diego Cupolo, "What Turkey's Election Observers Saw," *The Atlantic*, April 21, 2017.

34. Steven A. Cook, "Turkey's Elections: Partially Free, Fair, and Fake," *Council on Foreign Relations* (blog), June 25, 2018.

35. Palko Karasz, "Five Takeaways from Turkey's Election," *New York Times*, July 25, 2018.

36. Onur Ant, "On Eve of Turkey's Election, Only Erdoğan Gets TV Time." Bloomberg Politics, June 23, 2018.

37. Ted Galen Carpenter, "NATO's Worrisome Authoritarian Storm Clouds," *Mediterranean Quarterly* 26, no. 4 (December 2015): 37–48, https://object.cato.org/sites/cato.org/files/articles/mediterranean_quarterly-2015-carpenter-37-48.pdf; and Ivan Krastev, "Eastern Europe's Illiberal Revolution: The Long Road to Democratic Decline," *Foreign Affairs* (May-June 2018): 49–56.

38. White House, "Remarks by the President at Clinton Global Initiative," New York, NY, September 23, 2014.

39. Fidesz lost its supermajority in 2015 balloting, although it remained, by far, the largest party in Hungary's parliament. Moreover, the principal beneficiary of that change was the even more illiberal Jobbik Party, which became the second largest bloc.

40. Some of the changes were especially ominous. One required churches receiving public funding to "collaborate with the state for the public interest." Another amendment restricted political advertising during election campaigns to public (i.e., government-run) media. Most of those outlets are under the secure control of Orbán's political allies. Yet another amendment insisted that "free speech cannot be aimed at violating the dignity of the Hungarian nation"—a standard so vague that critics could be prosecuted virtually at will.

41. Pablo Gorondi, "Hungary's Leader Wants Drug Tests for Journalists," Associated Press, December 12, 2014.

42. Marc Santora, "George Soros-Founded University Is Forced Out of Hungary," *New York Times*, December 3, 2018.

43. Marton Dunai, "Multiculturalism Doesn't Work in Hungary, Says Orban," Reuters, June 3, 2015.

44. "Hungary's President Signs Disputed Asylum Law," Associated Press, March 16, 2017.

45. Maurits Meijers and Harmen van der Veer, "Hungary's Government Is Increasingly Autocratic. What Is the European Parliament Doing about It?," *Washington Post*, May 3, 2017; and George Szirtes, "Here Lies Danger. Hungary Is on the Verge of Full-Blown Autocracy," *The Guardian*, March 30, 2018.

46. Angela Dewan and Boglarka Kosztolanyi, "Hungary Is Starting to Look a Bit Like Russia. Here's Why," CNN.com, April 6, 2018.

47. "50,000 Rally in Warsaw to 'Defend Democracy,'" Agence France-Presse, December 12, 2015; and Rick Lyman and Joanna Berendt, "As Poland Lurches to the Right, Many in Europe Look on in Alarm," *New York Times*, December 14, 2015.

48. Piotr Skolimowski, "Poland Demands Apology after EU's Schultz Likens Changes to Coup," Bloomberg Business, December 15, 2015, https://www.bloomberg.com/news/articles/2015-12-14/poland-demands-apology-after-eu-s-schultz-likens-changes-to-coup?cmpid=yhoo.headline.

49. Brian Porter-Szücs, "Poland's Judicial Purge Another Step toward Authoritarian Democracy," *The Conversation*, July 6, 2018.

50. Porter-Szücs, "Poland's Judicial Purge."

51. Paul Waldie, "What Happened to Poland? How Poles Drifted from Europe into Populist Authoritarianism," *Globe and Mail*, January 24, 2018.

52. Molly O'Neal, "The European 'Other' in Poland's Conservative Identity Project," *International Spectator* 52, no. 1 (February 2017): 28–45.

53. O'Neal, "The European 'Other.'"

54. Ivan Krastev, "Eastern Europe's Illiberal Revolution," *Foreign Affairs* 97, no. 3 (May-June 2018): 49–56. Also see Celeste A. Wallander, "NATO's Enemies Within: How Democratic Decline Could Destroy the Alliance," *Foreign Affairs* 97, no. 4 (July-August 2018): 70–81. For earlier analyses warning of ominous trends, see Jan-Werner Mueller, "Eastern Europe Goes South: Disappearing Democracy in the EU's Newest Members," *Foreign Affairs* 93, no. 2 (March-April 2014): 14–19; and Cas Mudde, "Europe's Populist Surge," *Foreign Affairs* 95, no. 6 (November-December 2016): 26–30.

55. Dalibor Rohac, "Hungary and Poland Aren't Democratic. They're Authoritarian," *Foreign Policy*, February 5, 2018. Also see Volha Charnysh, "The Rise of Poland's Far Right: How Extremism Is Going Mainstream," *Foreign Affairs*, December 18, 2017.

56. Stanley Weiss, "It's Time to Kick Erdoğan's Turkey Out of NATO," *Huffington Post*, February 23, 2017; David A. Welch, "It's Time to Drum Increasingly Authoritarian Turkey out of NATO," *Globe and Mail*, April 22, 2018; Bernard-Henri Lévy, "NATO Should Give Turkey the Boot," *Wall Street Journal*, August 13, 2018; and Michael Rubin, "It's Time for Turkey and NATO to Go Their Separate Ways," *Washington Post*, August 16, 2018, https://www.washingtonpost.com/news/democracy-post/wp/2018/08/16/its-time-for-turkey-and-nato-to-go-their-separate-ways/?utm_term=.b6a8796f6d04.

57. "Turkey Signs Russian Missile Deal, Reportedly Worth $2.5 Billion," Radio Free Europe/Radio Liberty, December 29, 2017.

58. Richard Sisk, "NATO Warns Turkey of 'Consequences' for Buying Russian S-400 Missiles," Military.com, October 27, 2017.

59. "Russia, Turkey Sign Gas Pipeline Deal," Radio Free Europe/Radio Liberty, October 10, 2016; and "Turkish, Russian, Iranian Companies Ink $7 Billion Energy Deal," *Daily Sabah*, August 15, 2017.

60. "Turkey Blasts U.S. and EU Sanctions against Russia," *Duran*, August 11, 2017, http://theduran.com/turkey-blasts-us-eu-sanctions-russia/.

61. Wallander, "NATO's Enemies Within," p. 71.

62. Rob Berschinski, "The Threat within NATO," *The Atlantic*, April 7, 2018.

63. "Italian Minister Says Rome Will Oppose Extension of EU Sanctions on Russia," Radio Free Europe/Radio Liberty, October 18, 2018.

64. North Atlantic Treaty Organization, "Brussels Declaration on Transatlantic Security and Solidarity," press release no. (2018) 094, July 11, 2018.

Chapter Two

1. Jack F. Matlock Jr., "Who Is the Bully? The U.S. Has Treated Russia Like a Loser since the End of the Cold War," *Washington Post*, March 14, 2014.

2. John J. Mearsheimer, *The Great Delusion: Liberal Dreams and International Realities* (New Haven, CT: Yale University Press, 2018), p. 172.

3. George H. W. Bush and Brent Scowcroft, *A World Transformed* (New York: Alfred A. Knopf, 1998), pp. 242, 248–57, 268–69, 299–301.

4. James A. Baker III and Thomas M. DeFrank, *The Politics of Diplomacy: Revolution, War & Peace. 1989–1992* (New York: G. P. Putnam's Sons, 1995), pp. 230–32, 234–36, 258–59.

5. Bush and Scowcroft, *World Transformed*, pp. 281–82.

6. Bush and Scowcroft, *World Transformed*, p. 262. For a description of the various professed changes and assurances, see pp. 293–94.

7. Bush and Scowcroft, *World Transformed*, p. 274. Gorbachev raised the possibility of a Soviet application for NATO membership during a later negotiating session as well. See p. 282.

8. Bush and Scowcroft, *World Transformed*, p. 249.

9. Bush and Scowcroft, *World Transformed*, pp. 300, 301.

10. Bush and Scowcroft, *World Transformed*, p. 301.

11. Bush and Scowcroft, *World Transformed*, p. 253. Emphasis added.

12. See Joshua R. Itzkowitz Shifrinson, *Rising Titans, Falling Giants: How Great Powers Exploit Power Shifts* (Ithaca, NY: Cornell University Press, 2018). For his discussion of U.S. policy toward Moscow during the late 1980s and early 1990s, see pp. 119–59.

13. Mearsheimer, *Great Delusion*, p. 172.

14. Strobe Talbott, "Why NATO Should Grow," *New York Review of Books*, August 10, 1995.

15. Madeleine Albright (with Bill Woodward), *Madam Secretary: A Memoir* (New York: Miramax Books, 2003), p. 167.

16. Mearsheimer, *Great Delusion*, p. 283n4.

17. Albright (with Woodward), *Madame Secretary*, p. 252.

18. Albright (with Woodward), *Madame Secretary*, p. 251.

19. Condoleezza Rice, *No Higher Honor: A Memoir of My Years in Washington* (New York: Crown Publishers, 2011), pp. 668–69.

20. Uwe Klussman, Matthias Schepp, and Klaus Wiegrefe, "Did the West Break Its Promise to Moscow?" *Spiegel* (Online), November 26, 2009, http://www.spiegel.de/international/world/nato-s-eastward-expansion-did-the-west-break-its-promise-to-moscow-a-663315.html.

21. Mark Kramer, "The Myth of a No-NATO-Enlargement Pledge to Russia," *Washington Quarterly* 32, no. 2 (April 2009): 39–61.

22. Mary Elise Sarotte, "A Broken Promise? What the West Really Told Moscow about NATO Expansion," *Foreign Affairs* 93, no. 1 (September-October 2014): 91.

23. For a range of views, see Sarotte, "A Broken Promise?," pp. 90–97; John J. Mearsheimer, "Why the Ukraine Crisis Is the West's Fault," *Foreign Affairs* 93, no. 5 (September-October 2014): 77–89; Eric Zuesse, "How America Double-Crossed Russia and Shamed the West," *Strategic Culture*, September 10, 2015; Joshua R. I. Shifrinson, "Deal or No Deal? The End of the Cold War and the U.S. Offer to Limit NATO Expansion," *International Security* 40, no. 4 (Spring 2016): 7–44; and Mearsheimer, *Great Delusion*, pp. 171–72.

24. Klussman, Schepp, and Wiegrefe, "Did the West Break Its Promise to Moscow?"

25. Svetlana Savranskaya and Tom Blanton, "NATO Expansion: What Gorbachev Heard," *Briefing Book No. 613*, National Security Archive, December 12, 2017, https://nsarchive.gwu.edu/briefing-book/russia-programs/2017-12-12/nato-expansion-what-gorbachev-heard-western-leaders-early#.WjAX9r_XxYI.twitter. Also see Dave Majumdar, "Newly Declassified Documents: Gorbachev Told NATO Wouldn't Move Past East German Border," *National Interest* (Online), December 12, 2017.

26. Adam Twardowski, "Why NATO Isn't a Threat to Russia," *National Interest* (Online), September 22, 2016.

27. Thomas L. Friedman, "Foreign Affairs; Now a Word from X," *New York Times*, May 2, 1998.

28. Mearsheimer, *Great Delusion*, p. 172.

29. Bill Clinton, *My Life* (New York: Alfred A. Knopf, 2004), p. 637.

30. Clinton, *My Life*, p. 675.

31. Clinton, *My Life*, p. 750.

32. Steven Erlanger, "In a New Attack against NATO, Yeltsin Talks of a 'Conflagration of War,'" *New York Times*, September 9, 1995. See also "Yeltsin Sees War Threat in NATO Enlargement," *Jamestown Foundation Monitor* 1, no. 91 (September 8, 1995).

33. Luke Harding, "Bush Backs Ukraine and Georgia for NATO Membership," *The Guardian* (UK), April 1, 2008, https://www.theguardian.com/world/2008/apr/01/nato.georgia.

34. "NATO Rebuffs Bush on Ukraine, Georgia," CBS News, April 2, 2008.

35. Rice, *No Higher Honor*, p. 671.

36. George W. Bush, *Decision Points* (New York: Crown Books, 2010), pp. 430–31.

37. North Atlantic Treaty Organization, "Bucharest Summit Declaration Issued by the Heads of State and Government Participating in the Meeting of the North Atlantic Council in Bucharest," press release no. (2008) 049, April 3, 2008.

38. Adrian Blomfield and James Kirkup, "Stay Away, Vladimir Putin Tells NATO," *The Telegraph* (UK), April 5, 2008.

39. "NATO Denies Georgia and Ukraine," BBC News (UK), April 3, 2008.

40. White House, "Remarks by the Vice President and Georgian Prime Minister in a Joint Press Conference," August 1, 2017.

41. John Bolton, "NATO Is Still the Answer," *Weekly Standard*, May 5, 2014.

42. Zbigniew Brzezinski, "Confronting Russian Chauvinism," *American Interest*, June 24, 2014.

43. Luke Coffey, "NATO Membership for Georgia: In U.S. and European Interest," Heritage Foundation Special Report no. 199, January 29, 2018.

44. Damon Wilson and David J. Kramer, "Enlarge NATO to Ensure Peace," *New Atlanticist* (blog), Atlantic Council, August 7, 2018.

45. Talbott, "Why NATO Should Grow."

46. Talbott, "Why NATO Should Grow."

47. Mearsheimer, *Great Delusion*, p. 172.

48. Mearsheimer, *Great Delusion*, p. 178.

49. Clinton, *My Life*, pp. 569, 607, 637.

50. Clinton, *My Life*, p. 607.

51. Mearsheimer, *Great Delusion*, p. 178.

52. Andrew Hanna, "Senate Votes Overwhelmingly to Admit Montenegro to NATO," *Politico*, March 28, 2017.

53. Bush, *Decision Points*, p. 439.

54. White House, "Remarks by President Obama to the People of Estonia," Tallinn, Estonia, September 3, 2014.

55. Robert M. Gates, *Duty: Memoirs of a Secretary at War* (New York: Alfred A. Knopf, 2014), p. 157. Emphasis in original.

56. Charles Krauthammer, "The Unipolar Moment," *Foreign Affairs* 70, no. 1, America and the World 1990/91 (1990/1991): 23–33.

57. Christopher Layne, *The Peace of Illusions: American Grand Strategy from 1940 to the Present* (Ithaca, NY: Cornell University Press, 2006), pp. 105–13.

58. Layne, *Peace of Illusions*, p. 112.

59. Daniel Larison, "Another Pointless Round of NATO Expansion Awaits," *American Conservative*, September 17, 2018.

60. Robert W. Merry, "NATO Is a Danger, Not a Guarantor of Peace," *American Conservative*, January 18, 2019.

61. Quoted in Andrew Kirell, "John McCain: Rand Paul 'Is Now Working for Vladimir Putin,'" *Daily Beast*, March 15, 2017.

62. Daniel Larison, "McCain's Obnoxious Montenegro Outburst," *American Conservative*, March 15, 2017.

63. John Dale Grover, "Only Macedonians Can Decide If They Want to Join NATO," *National Interest* (Online), October 10, 2018.

64. When Yugoslavia broke up and Macedonia became independent in the 1990s, Athens objected to its use of that name because it also applies to a prominent region in Greece. Greeks believed that Skopje's stance on the name issue disrespected and undermined Greece's history, culture, and national identity. Some Greeks even worried that Skopje's appropriation of the name was the opening stage of an expansionist agenda. A clunky compromise using the name "Former Yugoslav Republic of Macedonia" (FYROM) gave Skopje some space to participate in international institutions, but Athens steadfastly blocked NATO or EU membership until a better solution could be reached. That finally happened in 2018 when the two countries agreed that FYROM's new name would be the Republic of North Macedonia.

65. U.S. Department of State, "Macedonia's Referendum on the Prespa Agreement," press release, September 30, 2018.

66. Krisztina Than, "NATO Should Press Ahead with Enlargement, CEE Countries Say," Reuters, February 25, 2016.

67. Poland, Ministry of Foreign Affairs, "Minister Witold Waszczykowski on Polish Diplomacy Priorities in 2017," February 9, 2017.

68. Republic of Latvia, Ministry of Foreign Affairs, "Statement by the Ministry of Foreign Affairs on Marking Ten Years since Russia's Aggression against Georgia," August 7, 2018.

69. "Ukraine, Georgia Should Become NATO Members—Latvian FM," *Ukrinform* (UA), August 7, 2018.

70. "France Doesn't Want Ukraine in NATO, Plans No Arms Supply to Kiev—Hollande," *TASS* (RU), February 5, 2015, http://tass.com/world/775625.

71. Nolan Peterson, "NATO Backs Free Ukraine. Only France Is Out of Step," *Newsweek*, July 11, 2016.

72. Quoted in "France, Germany against Ukraine, Georgia, Moldova Joining NATO—French MP," *Sputnik* (RU), December 5, 2015.

73. Christoph Schult, "Stop Talking about NATO Membership for Ukraine," *Spiegel* (Online; DE), December 2, 2014.

74. Kenneth Rapoza, "Ukraine's NATO Pipe Dream?" *Forbes*, September 19, 2017.

75. "Why People Are Worried about Trump's Montenegro Comments," CBS News, July 19, 2018.

76. Dimitri K. Simes, "Trouble with Russia," *National Interest*, no. 144 (July-August 2016): 9.

Chapter Three

1. Paul Starobin, "Kremlin Caricature," *National Interest*, no. 141 (January-February 2016): 48–52.

2. Joe Gould, "U.S. Senate's Top Republican Likens Russia to 'Old Soviet Union,'" *Defense News*, August 15, 2018.

3. Donald Rumsfeld, *Known and Unknown: A Memoir* (New York: Sentinel, 2011), p. 540.

4. David Goldfischer, "'Peace for Our Time?' Helsinki 2018 and Munich 1938," *Denver Post*, July 16, 2018.

5. Chuck Ross, "Ex-CIA Director John Brennan Accuses Trump of Treason Following Putin Summit," *Daily Caller*, July 16, 2018; and Mike Lillis, "Hoyer: Trump Committed 'Treason' in Helsinki," *The Hill*, July 17, 2018.

6. "Zakaria on Trump: 'Treasonous' Too Weak a Word," CNN Wire, July 17, 2018, http://www.wtva.com/content/national/488395071.html.

7. Mark Hertling and Molly K. McKew, "Putin's Attack on the U.S. Is Our Pearl Harbor," *Politico*, July 16, 2018.

8. Ian Schwartz, "Friedman: Flynn Resignation Shows Russia Hacking Was on Scale with 9/11, Pearl Harbor," *RealClearPolitics*, February 14, 2017.

9. Morgan Chalfant, "Democrats Step Up Calls That Russia Hack Was Act of War," *The Hill*, March 26, 2017.

10. Daniel McCarthy, "Why the House Hearings Revealed More about America Than Russia," *National Interest* (Online), March 20, 2017.

11. Chalfant, "Democrats Step Up Calls."

12. Richard C. Young, "Conspiracy and Collusion with Russia?" Richardcyoung.com, February 20, 2018.

13. Nina Agrawal, "The U.S. Is No Stranger to Interfering in the Elections of Other Countries," *Los Angeles Times*, December 21, 2016; and Ishaan Tharoor, "The Long History of the U.S. Interfering in Elections Elsewhere," *Washington Post*, October 3, 2016.

14. Eleanor Randolph, "Americans Claim Role in Yeltsin Win," *Los Angeles Times*, July 9, 1996.

15. Greg Olear, "Red Paul: The Senator from Kentucky Is Now Working for Vladimir Putin," *Medium*, January 1, 2019.

16. For examples of such smears, see Peter Beinart, "Donald Trump's Defenders on the Left," *The Atlantic*, July 23, 2017; Nicholas Grossman, "Why Are Internet Radicals Helping Putin's Russia?" *ARC*, July 21, 2018; and Alexander Reid Ross, "How Assad's War Crimes Bring Far Left and Right Together—Under Putin's Benevolent Gaze," *Haaretz* (IL), April 17, 2018. Such tactics began long before Donald Trump became the favorite target of Russophobes. Some date from the Ukraine tensions in 2014. For a typical example, see Jonathan Chait, "The Pathetic Lives of Putin's American Dupes," *New York Magazine*, March 14, 2014. Critics of the new McCarthyism have not remained silent. See Glenn Greenwald, "Democrats' Tactic of Accusing Critics of Kremlin Allegiance Has Long, Ugly History in U.S." *The Intercept*, August 8, 2016; and Ted Galen Carpenter, "Why Democrats Are Obsessed with Russia, *National Interest* (blog), February 9, 2018, https://www.cato.org/publications/commentary/why-democrats-are-obsessed-russia.

17. Glenn Greenwald, "A Consensus Emerges: Russia Committed an 'Act of War' on Par with Pearl Harbor and 9/11: Should the U.S. Response Be Similar?," *The Intercept*, February 19, 2018.

18. Office of Senator John McCain, "SASC [Senate Armed Services Committee] Chairman John McCain on Trump-Putin Meeting," press release, July 16, 2018.

19. Dan Balz, "The Moment Called for Trump to Stand Up for America. He Chose to Bow," *Washington Post*, July 16, 2018.

20. Jack F. Matlock Jr., "Who Is the Bully? The U.S. Has Treated Russia Like a Loser since the End of the Cold War," *Washington Post*, March 14, 2014.

21. Richard K. Betts, "The Lost Logic of Deterrence," *Foreign Affairs* 92, no. 2 (March-April 2013): 90.

22. Gregory L. Freeze, "Russian Orthodoxy and Politics in the Putin Era," White Paper, *Carnegie Endowment for International Peace*, February 9, 2017.

23. Neil Buckley, "Putin Urges Russians to Return to Values of Religion," *Financial Times*, September 19, 2013, https://www.ft.com/content/cdedfd64-214f-11e3-a92a-00144feab7de.

24. Joseph R. Biden Jr. and Michael Carpenter, "How to Stand Up to the Kremlin," *Foreign Affairs* 97, no. 1 (January-February 2018): 45.

25. Ted Galen Carpenter, *Gullible Superpower: U.S. Support for Bogus Foreign Democratic Movements* (Washington: Cato Institute, 2019). See especially chapters 5 and 9.

26. Michael McFaul, "Russia as It Is," *Foreign Affairs* 97, no. 4 (July-August 2018): 82. For a more sophisticated version of the thesis that Russia is trying to orchestrate an alternative to the existing "liberal international order" in which Moscow would play a more prominent and influential role, see Mamuka Tsereteli, "Can Russia's Quest for the New International Order Succeed?," *Orbis* 62, no. 2 (Spring 2018): 204–19.

27. Mac Margolis, "Russia Wants to Be Latin America's New BFF," Bloomberg, September 18, 2017; and Magnus Lindstrom, "Why Are U.S. Allies Japan and South Korea Drawing Closer to Russia?," *The Diplomat*, March 20, 2018, https://thediplomat.com/2018/03/why-are-us-allies-japan-and-south-korea-drawing-closer-to-russia/.

28. Carpenter, *Gullible Superpower*, pp. 194–205; Richard Sakwa, *Frontline Ukraine: Crisis in the Borderlands* (London: I. B. Tauris, 2015); Samuel Charap and Timothy J. Colton, *Everyone Loses: The Ukraine Crisis and the Ruinous Contest for Post-Soviet Eurasia* (London: Routledge, 2017); and John J. Mearsheimer, "Why the Ukraine Crisis Is the West's Fault," *Foreign Affairs* 93, no. 5 (September-October 2014): 77–89.

29. Sam Greene and Graeme Robertson, "Explaining Putin's Popularity: Rallying Round the Russian Flag," *Washington Post*, September 9, 2014.

30. Russia did also sign the Budapest Memorandum in 1994, pledging to respect Ukraine's territorial integrity as part of the process whereby Kiev relinquished possession of the nuclear weapons it had inherited when the Soviet Union dissolved. But the memorandum was merely a statement of diplomatic policy by the signatory parties at that time. It was not a binding treaty ratified by the Russian Duma—or, for that matter, the United States Senate. Executive agreements that U.S. presidents conclude with foreign leaders likewise can be altered or abolished at any time by that chief executive or a successor. Russia's actions in 2014 may have been less than honorable, but they did not violate a formal treaty.

31. Daniel Treisman, "Why Putin Took Crimea: The Gambler in the Kremlin," *Foreign Affairs* 95, no. 3 (May-June 2016): 47.

32. Peter Walker, "Russian Expansionism May Pose Existential Threat, Says NATO General," *The Guardian* (UK), February 20, 2015.

33. Curt Mills, "Panetta: Putin Wants to Restore the Soviet Union," *U.S. News*, December 1, 2016.

34. "McCain: Putin Wants 'to Restore Old Russian Empire,'" *Political Ticker . . .*, CNN Politics, August 12, 2008.

35. Andrei Shleifer and Daniel Treisman, "Why Moscow Says No," *Foreign Affairs* 90, no. 1 (January-February 2011): 129.

36. Philip M. Breedlove, "NATO's Next Act," *Foreign Affairs* 95, no. 4 (July-August 2016): 98.

37. Nearly two weeks after passage of the resolution and commencement of the aircraft and missile attacks, President Obama still sought to portray the mission as a limited one to protect innocent civilians: White House, "Remarks by the President in Address to the Nation on Libya," National Defense University, Washington, March 28, 2011.

38. Indeed, in 2012, she was still trying to sell Russian Foreign Minister Sergei Lavrov on endorsing a UN resolution authorizing a similar "limited"

intervention in Syria. The Russians, she noted ruefully, "weren't having any of it." Hillary Clinton, *Hard Choices* (New York: Simon and Schuster, 2014), p. 451.

39. Robert M. Gates, *Duty: Memoirs of a Secretary at War* (New York: Alfred A. Knopf, 2014), p. 530.

40. Ted Galen Carpenter, "Washington's UN Temper Tantrum," *National Interest* (Online), February 6, 2012, https://www.cato.org/publications/commentary/washingtons-un-temper-tantrum.

41. "Syria Veto 'Outrageous' Says UN Envoy Susan Rice," NPR, February 5, 2012, https://www.npr.org/2012/02/05/146424981/un-ambassador-susan-rice-fumes-at-syria-veto.

42. "Syria: Hillary Clinton Calls Russia and China 'Despicable' for Opposing UN Resolution," *The Telegraph* (UK), February 25, 2012.

43. Ralph Peters, "Putin's Plan to Reclaim the Old Soviet Empire," *New York Post*, May 3, 2014.

44. Pavlo Klimkin, "Putin's Desire for a New Russian Empire Won't Stop with Ukraine," *The Guardian* (UK), March 25, 2017.

45. "Russia Extends Belligerence toward Ukraine with Aggression at Sea," *Rachel Maddow Show*, MSNBC, November 26, 2018, https://www.msnbc.com/rachel-maddow/watch/russia-extends-belligerence-toward-ukraine-with-aggression-at-sea-1381251651698.

46. Thomas Escritt and Andrew Osborn, "Ukrainian Leader Says Putin Wants His Whole Country," Reuters, November 29, 2018.

47. Carol Morello, "U.N. Ambassador Nikki Haley Condemns Russia's 'Outlaw' Actions against Ukrainian Ships," *Washington Post*, November 26, 2018.

48. Daniel Hoffman, "U.S., Allies Must Check Putin's Latest Move against Ukraine," *The Hill*, November 28, 2018, https://thehill.com/opinion/international/418633-us-allies-must-check-putins-latest-move-against-ukraine.

49. Christine Maza, "Russia vs. Ukraine War: This Is How West Would Respond to Russian Invasion," *Newsweek*, November 27, 2018.

50. For an interesting and informative discussion of the competing explanations for Putin's decision to annex Crimea and how planned or spontaneous that decision was, see Treisman, "Why Putin Took Crimea," pp. 47–54.

51. Philip Rucker, "Hillary Clinton Says Putin's Actions Are Like 'What Hitler Did Back in the 30s,'" *Washington Post*, March 5, 2014.

52. Quoted in Lally Weymouth, "'Russia Is a Threat': Estonia Frets about Its Neighbor," *Washington Post*, March 24, 2017.

53. Henry Foy and Stefan Wagstyl, "Angela Merkel Says Russia Damaging Europe's Security," *Financial Times*, July 7, 2016.

54. Embassy of the Republic of Latvia in Hungary, "Interview of the Minister of Foreign Affairs of Latvia to the Weekly Newspaper *HVG*," January 20, 2017.

55. Lally Weymouth, "'Russia Is a Threat . . . to All of Europe," *Foreign Policy*, March 24, 2017.

56. "Polish Minister Says Russia More Dangerous Than ISIS," Radio Free Europe/Radio Liberty, April 18, 2016, https://www.rferl.org/a/polish-minister-says-russia-more-dangerous-than-islamic-state/27677667.html.

57. Rob Smith, "The World's Biggest Economies in 2018," World Economic Forum, April 18, 2018.

58. César Chelala, "Public Health: Russia Is Sick," *The Globalist*, October 3, 2015.

59. Dave Majumdar, "The Rise of Russia's Military," *National Interest* no. 156 (July-August 2018): 36–46; and Dmitri Trenin, "The Revival of the Russian Military," *Foreign Affairs* 95, no. 3 (May-June 2016): 23–29.

60. Lucie Beraud-Sudreau, "On the Up: Western defence spending in 2018," *Military Balance* (blog), February 15, 2019. *Military Balance* uses a fairly narrow definition of military spending. The most generally accepted figure in the press for U.S. "defense" spending in 2018, for example, is $716 billion.

61. Rajeswari Pillai Rajagopalan, "China's Military Budget: New Numbers, Old Worries," *The Diplomat*, March 7, 2018.

62. Rick Noack, "Even As Fear of Russia Is Rising, Its Military Spending Is Actually Decreasing," *Washington Post*, May 2, 2018.

63. John Mueller, "Nuclear Weapons Don't Matter," *Foreign Affairs* 97, no. 6 (November-December 2018): 10–15. https://www.cato.org/publications/commentary/nuclear-weapons-dont-matter.

64. Dimitri K. Simes, "Trouble with Russia," *National Interest* no. 144 (July-August 2016): 5.

65. Betts, "Lost Logic of Deterrence," p. 90.

66. Betts, "Lost Logic of Deterrence," p. 88.

67. Matt Spetalnick, "Bush: Missile Shield Is Meant to Deter Iran," Reuters, October 23, 2007, https://www.reuters.com/article/us-bush-shield-idUSWAT00833920071023; and "Bush: Missile Shield No Threat to Russia," CNN.com, April 1, 2008, http://www.cnn.com/2008/POLITICS/04/01/bush.nato/.

68. "Iran Increases Testing of Ballistic Missiles That Can Reach Europe," *Jerusalem Post* (IL), December 9, 2018.

69. The Obama administration abandoned plans for the missile shield in 2009 but revived them in 2016. Ryan Browne, "U.S. Launches Long-Awaited European Defense Shield," CNN.com, May 12, 2016. On the latter occasion, U.S. leaders still clung to the fiction that the system was directed at Iran, not Russia. Jamie McIntyre, "Pentagon: U.S. Missile Shield in Romania Aimed at Iran, Not Russia," *Washington Examiner*, May 12, 2016.

70. Gates, *Duty*, p. 155.

71. Gates, *Duty*, p. 155.

72. Gates, *Duty*, pp. 157, 158.

73. Gates, *Duty*, p. 158.

74. See, for example, Eugene B. Rumer, Richard Sokolsky, and Andrew S. Weiss, "Trump and Russia: The Right Way to Manage Relations," *Foreign Affairs* 96, no. 2 (March-April 2017): 12–19.

75. Robert W. Merry, "NATO Is a Danger, Not a Guarantor of Peace," *American Conservative*, January 18, 2019.

Chapter Four

1. Doug Bandow, "America's Facebook Friend Allies," *American Conservative*, August 16, 2018, https://www.cato.org/publications/commentary/americas-facebook-friend-allies.

2. "Why People Are Worried about Trump's Montenegro Comments," CBS News, July 19, 2018.

3. Doug Bandow, "Would You Send Your Son or Daughter to Die for Montenegro?" *National Interest* (Online), July 30, 2018, https://www.cato.org/publications/commentary/would-you-send-son-or-daughter-die-montenegro.

4. Predrag Milic, "Montenegro to Russia: 'Keep Your Hands Off' Our NATO Bid," AP News, February 14, 2017; and Steve Holland, "U.S. Says 'Credible Reports' Russia Tried to Interfere with Montenegro's Elections," Reuters, April 12, 2017.

5. "Kosovo Parliament Passes Border Deal Despite Tear Gas," Radio Free Europe/Radio Liberty, March 21, 2018.

6. Ted Galen Carpenter, "Waist Deep in the Balkans and Sinking: Washington Confronts the Crisis in Macedonia," Cato Institute Policy Analysis no. 317, April 30, 2001, https://object.cato.org/sites/cato.org/files/pubs/pdf/pa397.pdf.

7. Sinisa Jakov Marusic, "Macedonia Albanians Rally against Government," *Balkan Insight*, April 22, 2016.

8. "Macedonian President Warns of Albanian Threat to Sovereignty," Voice of America, March 7, 2017; and "Macedonia Accuses Albania of Interfering in Internal Affairs," Radio Free Europe/Radio Liberty, April 4, 2017.

9. "Macedonian President Refuses Again to Sign Bill Boosting Albanian Language," Radio Free Europe/Radio Liberty, March 15, 2018.

10. Jerry Hendrix, "When Putin Invades the Baltics," *National Review*, February 5, 2018; and Molly K. McKew, "'They Will Die in Tallinn': Estonia Girds for War with Russia," *Politico*, July 10, 2018.

11. Robert Coalson, "Putin Pledges to Defend All Ethnic Russians Anywhere. So, Where Are They?," Radio Free Europe/Radio Liberty, April 10, 2014; and Julian Borger and Luke Harding, "Baltic States Wary as Russia Takes More Strident Tone with Neighbors," *The Guardian* (UK), September 18, 2014.

12. Doug Bandow, "Why on Earth Would Russia Attack the Baltics?," *National Interest* (Online), February 7, 2016, https://www.cato.org/publications/commentary/why-earth-would-russia-attack-baltics.

13. David A. Shlapak and Michael Johnson, *Reinforcing Deterrence on NATO's Eastern Flank: Wargaming the Defense of the Baltics* (Washington: RAND Corporation, 2016). Also see Dave Majumdar, "Revealed: Russian Invasion Could Overrun NATO in 60 Hours," *National Interest* (Online), February 4, 2016.

14. Mark Galeotti, "Why Did It Take Turkey Just 17 Seconds to Shoot Down Russian Jet?," *The Guardian* (UK), November 26, 2015.

15. Jacob Bojesson, "Turkey Violated Greek Airspace 2,244 Times Last Year, Fires at Russia for Doing It Once," *Daily Caller*, November 24, 2015.

16. Tuvan Gumrukca and Ece Toksabay, "Turkey, Russia Sign Deal on Supply of S-400 Missiles," Reuters, December 29, 2017.

17. "Crossing the Line: Georgia's Violent Dispersal of Protestors and Raid on Imedi Television," *Human Rights Watch* 19, no. 8(D) (December 2007): 6.

18. Luke Harding, "Bush Backs Ukraine and Georgia for NATO Membership," *The Guardian* (UK), April 1, 2008.

19. "NATO Rebuffs Bush on Ukraine, Georgia," CBS News, April 2, 2008.

20. Robert M. Gates, *Duty: Memoirs of a Secretary at War* (New York: Alfred A. Knopf, 2014), p. 167.

21. George W. Bush, *Decision Points* (New York: Crown Books, 2010), pp. 434–35.

22. Nathan Hodge, "Did the U.S. Prep Georgia for War with Russia?" *Wired*, August 8, 2008.

23. Bush, *Decision Points*, p. 435.

24. Robert Stacy McCain, "McCain: We Are All Georgians Now," *American Spectator*, August 12, 2008, https://spectator.org/14931_mccain-we-are-all-georgians-now/.

25. Bush, *Decision Points*, p. 435.

26. Terri Moon Cronk, "U.S. Troops Training Ukrainian Soldiers, Mattis Says," Department of Defense News, February 2, 2018.

27. Christopher Miller, "U.S. Confirms Delivery of Javelin Antitank Missiles to Ukraine," Radio Free Europe/Radio Liberty, April 30, 2018.

28. Carol Morello and David Filipov, "Russia Issues Stern Warning U.S. Is Fueling New Bloodshed in Ukraine," *Washington Post*, December 23, 2017.

29. Julian Borger, "U.S. Ready to Boost Arms Supplies to Ukraine Naval and Air Forces, Envoy Says," *The Guardian* (UK), September 1, 2018.

30. Quoted in Borger, "U.S. Ready to Boost Arms Supplies."

31. "Russia-Ukraine Tensions Rise after Kerch Strait Ship Capture," BBC News (UK), November 26, 2018.

32. "NATO Convenes Emergency Meeting with Ukraine over Russian Seizure of Vessels," Reuters, November 26, 2018.

33. Jonathan Marcus, "Ukraine-Russia Sea Clash: Poroshenko Urges NATO to Send Ships," BBC News (UK), November 29, 2018.

34. Mamuka Tsereteli, "Can Russia's Quest for the New International Order Succeed?" *Orbis* 62, no. 2 (Spring 2018): 215–16, 219.

35. Joe Gould, "U.S. Lawmakers Urge Trump to Arm Ukraine, Break Silence on Russian Blockade," *Defense News*, November 26, 2018.

36. Joe Gould, "U.S., Ukraine in 'Close Discussion' for New Lethal Arms," *Defense News*, November 18, 2018.

37. Quoted in Nolan Peterson, "Trump Bolsters European Defenses against Putin," *Newsweek*, May 29, 2017.

38. Justin Sink, "Poland Offers 'Fort Trump' as Name If U.S. Builds Base," Bloomberg, September 18, 2018.

39. Daniel Larison, "There Is No Need for a U.S. Military Base in Poland," *American Conservative*, September 18, 2018.

40. An especially terrifying incident occurred in September 1983, but a Soviet officer declined to follow the usual protocol to launch the USSR's strategic missiles on warning if radar showed an incoming U.S. missile strike. A less diligent individual might have given the fateful order, even though the radar images ultimately proved erroneous. See Kristine Phillips, "The Former Soviet Officer Who Trusted His Gut—and Averted a Global Nuclear Catastrophe," *Washington Post*, September 18, 2017.

41. Ivo H. Daalder, "Responding to Russia's Resurgence," *Foreign Affairs* 94, no. 6 (November-December 2017): 37–38.

Chapter Five

1. Madeleine Albright, interview by Matt Lauer, *The Today Show*, NBC-TV, Columbus, OH, February 19, 1998, as released by the U.S. Department of State.

2. George H. W. Bush and Brent Scowcroft, *A World Transformed* (New York: Alfred A. Knopf, 1998), p. 301.

3. Jolyon Howorth and John T. S. Keeler, "The EU, NATO, and the Quest for European Autonomy," in *Defending Europe: The EU, NATO, and the Quest for European Autonomy*, ed. Jolyon Howorth and John T. S. Keeler (New York: Palgrave Macmillan, 2002), p. 7.

4. North Atlantic Treaty Organization, "The Alliance's Strategic Concept," press release NAC-S(99)65, April 24, 1999, paragraph 30. For a discussion of NATO's new strategic concept and the divisions among the various factions regarding the alliance's appropriate future mission, see Ted Galen Carpenter, "NATO's New Strategic Concept: Coherent Blueprint or Conceptual Muddle,"

in *NATO Enters the 21st Century,* ed. Ted Galen Carpenter (London: Frank Cass Publishers, 2001), pp. 7–28; see especially pp. 12–16.

5. Stuart Croft et al., "NATO's Triple Challenge," *International Affairs* 76, no. 3 (July 2000): 496–518.

6. Christopher Layne, *The Peace of Illusions: American Grand Strategy from 1940 to the Present* (Ithaca, NY: Cornell University Press, 2006), p. 113.

7. Layne, *Peace of Illusions*, pp. 113–14. For a broader discussion of U.S. hostility to the ESDP and European-U.S. disagreements and tensions regarding the issue, see Moritz Weiss, *Transaction Costs and Security Institutions: Unravelling the ESDP* (New York: Palgrave Macmillan, 2011).

8. Douglas Hamilton and Charles Aldinger, "EU Force Could Spell NATO's End, Cohen Says," *Washington Post*, December 6, 2000.

9. Layne, *Peace of Illusions*, p. 114.

10. Quoted in Layne, *Peace of Illusions*, p. 114.

11. Layne, *Peace of Illusions*, p. 114.

12. U.S. Department of State, "Secretary of State Madeleine K. Albright Statement to the North Atlantic Council," Brussels, Belgium, December 8, 1998.

13. Judy Dempsey, "U.S. Seeks Showdown with EU over NATO," *Financial Times*, October 17, 2003.

14. Condoleezza Rice, *No Higher Honor: A Memoir of My Years in Washington* (New York: Crown Publishers, 2011), p. 39.

15. Donald Rumsfeld, *Known and Unknown: A Memoir* (New York: Sentinel, 2011), p. 444.

16. Rumsfeld, *Known and Unknown*, p. 444.

17. David M. Herszenhorn, "EU Vows to Thwart Trump's Sanctions on Iran," *Politico*, August 13, 2018.

18. World Bank, "Gross Domestic Product 2017," World Development Indicators Database, January 25, 2019, http://databank.worldbank.org/data/download/GDP.pdf.

19. International Monetary Fund, "GDP, Current Prices," IMF DataMapper, October 2018.

20. Lucie Beraud-Sudreau, "On the Up: Western defence spending in 2018," *Military Balance* (blog), February 15, 2019.

21. "Russian Military Spending Falls, Could Affect Operations: Think-Tank," Reuters, May 1, 2018.

22. James Hackett, ed., "Turkey," *The Military Balance 2018* 188, no.1 (February 2018): 156–59.

23. Hackett, ed., "Germany," *Military Balance 2018*, pp. 107–10.

24. Hackett, ed., "Poland," *Military Balance 2018*, pp. 135–37.

25. Hackett, ed., "France," *Military Balance 2018*, pp. 102–07.

26. Hackett, ed., "United Kingdom," *Military Balance 2018*, pp. 160–65.

27. Michaela Dodge, "U.S. Nuclear Weapons in Europe: Critical for Transatlantic Security," Heritage Foundation Backgrounder no. 2875, February 18, 2014.

28. Todd S. Sechser and Matthew Fuhrmann, *Nuclear Weapons and Coercive Diplomacy* (New York: Cambridge University Press, 2017). Also see John Mueller, "Nuclear Weapons Don't Matter," *Foreign Affairs* 97, no. 6 (November–December 2018): 10–15, https://www.cato.org/publications/commentary/nuclear-weapons-dont-matter.

29. Stockholm International Peace Research Institute, *SIPRI Yearbook 2018: Armaments, Disarmaments, and International Security* (New York: Oxford University Press, 2018), p. 236.

30. Matthew Karnitschnig, "German Bomb Debate Goes Nuclear," *Politico*, August 13, 2018; Rudolph Herzog, "German Nukes Would Be a National Tragedy," *Foreign Policy*, March 10, 2017; Maximilian Terhalle, "If Germany Goes Nuclear, Blame Trump before Putin," *Foreign Policy*, April 3, 2017; and Christian Hacke, "Why Germany Should Get the Bomb," *National Interest* (Online), August 12, 2018.

31. Herzog, "German Nukes Would be a National Tragedy."

32. See especially Kenneth Waltz, "The Spread of Nuclear Weapons: More May Be Better," *Adelphi Papers*, no. 171 (London: International Institute for Strategic Studies, 1981).

33. "Visegrad Countries Urge EU to Build a Common Army," *Deutsche Welle* (GER), August 26, 2016.

34. Benjamin Kentish, "Emmanuel Macron Calls for EU Army and Shared Defence Budget," *The Independent* (UK), September 26, 2017.

35. Romina McGuinness, "EU Army? Macron Proposes 'European NATO' to Free Bloc from Reliance on U.S.," *Express* (UK), August 31, 2018, https://www.express.co.uk/news/world/1011362/france-news-emmanuel-macron-european-nato-EU-Army.

36. Justin Huggler, "Merkel Voices Support for Macron's Proposed European Defence Force," *The Telegraph* (UK), June 3, 2018.

37. David M. Herszenhorn, Lili Bayer, and Jacopo Barigazzi, "EU, Founded as Project of Peace, Plans Military Future," *Politico*, August 30, 2018, updated January 15, 2019.

38. Herszenhorn, Bayer, and Barigazzi, "EU, Founded as Project of Peace."

39. European Parliament, "Annual Report on the Implementation of the Common Security and Defence Policy," Strasbourg, texts adopted December 13, 2017.

40. Kevin Ruane, *The Rise and Fall of the European Defence Community* (London: Palgrave Macmillan, 2000).

41. European Commission, "EU Budget: Stepping up the EU's Role as a Security and Defence Provider," press release, June 13, 2018.

42. Herszenhorn, Bayer, and Barigazzi, "EU, Founded as Project of Peace."

43. John Bolton, "Donald Trump Has a Point about NATO," *Boston Globe*, September 27, 2016.

44. Ironically, some NATO traditionalists in Europe were already making that distinction quite emphatically in the 1990s, worried that European members might be drawn into U.S. conflicts or problems in Latin America, East Asia, or elsewhere. See Carpenter, "NATO's New Strategic Concept," pp. 10–12.

45. Quoted in William Drozdiak, "European Allies Balk at Expanded Role for NATO," *Washington Post*, February 22, 1998.

46. Warren Christopher and William J. Perry, "NATO's True Mission," *New York Times*, October 21, 1997.

47. Quoted in Craig R. Whitney, "Europe Looks Quizzically at U.S. Proposal for NATO Strategy," *New York Times*, December 9, 1998.

48. John-Thor Dahlburg, "NATO Ponders New Role as It Nears 50," *Los Angeles Times*, December 9, 1998.

49. Henry Kissinger, "No U.S. Ground Forces for Kosovo," *Washington Post*, February 2, 1999.

50. Martin Egnash, "U.S. Soldiers Deploy to Kosovo amid Enduring Tensions," *Stars and Stripes*, July 13, 2017.

51. Richard Wike, "Where Americans and Europeans Agree, Disagree on Foreign Policy," Pew Research Center, June 24, 2016.

Conclusion

1. Earl C. Ravenal, "The Case for Strategic Disengagement," *Foreign Affairs* 51, no. 3 (April 1973): 504–21.

2. George Washington, "Farewell Address" (1796), ourdocuments.gov. https://www.ourdocuments.gov/doc.php?flash=false&doc=15.

3. Robert A. Taft, *A Foreign Policy for Americans* (New York: Doubleday, 1951).

4. For example, see Julian E. Barnes and Helene Cooper, "Trump Discussed Pulling U.S. from NATO, Aides Say amid New Concerns over Russia," *New York Times*, January 14, 2019. For a firm rebuttal of the arguments that NATO must continue forever, see Robert W. Merry, "NATO Is a Danger, Not a Guarantor of Peace," *American Conservative*, January 18, 2019."

5. James Stavridis, "I Once Led NATO: President Trump's Talk of Leaving Will Make Only Putin Happy," *Time*, January 18, 2019.

6. Jeff Gerth and Tim Weiner, "Arms Makers See Bonanza in Selling NATO Expansion," *New York Times*, June 29, 1997.

7. Ted Galen Carpenter, "Accepting Spheres of Influence in the 21st Century," *Aspenia* Online (IT), May 7, 2014, https://www.cato.org/publications/commentary/accepting-spheres-influence-21st-century.

8. U.S. Department of State, "Secretary Rice Addresses U.S.-Russia Relations at the German Marshall Fund," Washington, September 18, 2008.

9. Ted Galen Carpenter, "Trump Didn't Wreck the 'Liberal International Order': It Never Really Existed to Begin With," *National Interest* (Online), November 17, 2018, https://www.cato.org/publications/commentary/trump-didnt-wreck-liberal-international-order.

10. Daniel Larison, "There Is No Case for U.S. Support for the War in Yemen," *American Conservative* (Online), August 6, 2018.

11. Roger Cohen, "China's Monroe Doctrine," *New York Times*, May 8, 2014; and Steven Jackson, "Does China Have a Monroe Doctrine? Evidence for Regional Exclusion," *Strategic Studies Quarterly* 10, no. 4 (Winter 2016): 64–89.

12. Claudia Grisales, "House Lawmakers Approve New NATO Protections," *Stars and Stripes*, January 22, 2019.

13. Ted Galen Carpenter, "Delusions of Indispensability," *National Interest* no. 124 (March-April 2013): 47–55, https://object.cato.org/sites/cato.org/files/articles/carpenter124.pdf.

14. For some of the scholarly treatments generally reflecting a grand strategy of realism and restraint, see Christopher A. Preble, *The Power Problem: How American Military Dominance Makes Us Less Safe, Less Prosperous, and Less Free* (Ithaca, NY: Cornell University Press, 2009); Barry R. Posen, *Restraint: A New Foundation for U.S. Grand Strategy* (Ithaca, NY: Cornell University Press, 2014); Walter A. McDougall, *The Tragedy of U.S. Foreign Policy: How American Civil Religion Betrayed the National Interest* (New Haven, CT: Yale University Press, 2016); John J. Mearsheimer, *The Great Delusion: Liberal Dreams and International Realities* (New Haven, CT: Yale University Press, 2018); Christopher Layne, *The Peace of Illusions: American Grand Strategy from 1940 to the Present* (Ithaca, NY: Cornell University Press, 2006); and A. Trevor Thrall and Benjamin H. Friedman, eds., *U.S. Grand Strategy in the 21st Century: The Case for Restraint* (New York: Routledge, 2018).

INDEX

Note: Information in notes is indicated by n.

ABOUT THE AUTHOR

Ted Galen Carpenter is senior fellow for defense and foreign policy studies at the Cato Institute. He is the author of 12 books on international affairs, including *Gullible Superpower: U.S. Support for Bogus Foreign Democratic Movements; The Fire Next Door: Mexico's Drug Violence and the Danger to America*; *Smart Power: Toward a Prudent Foreign Policy for America*; and *The Captive Press: Foreign Policy Crises and the First Amendment.* Dr. Carpenter is also the editor of 10 books and the author of more than 800 articles on security issues.

Cato Institute

Founded in 1977, the Cato Institute is a public policy research foundation dedicated to broadening the parameters of policy debate to allow consideration of more options that are consistent with the principles of limited government, individual liberty, and peace. To that end, the Institute strives to achieve greater involvement of the intelligent, concerned lay public in questions of policy and the proper role of government.

The Institute is named for *Cato's Letters*, libertarian pamphlets that were widely read in the American Colonies in the early 18th century and played a major role in laying the philosophical foundation for the American Revolution.

Despite the achievement of the nation's Founders, today virtually no aspect of life is free from government encroachment. A pervasive intolerance for individual rights is shown by government's arbitrary intrusions into private economic transactions and its disregard for civil liberties. And while freedom around the globe has notably increased in the past several decades, many countries have moved in the opposite direction, and most governments still do not respect or safeguard the wide range of civil and economic liberties.

To address those issues, the Cato Institute undertakes an extensive publications program on the complete spectrum of policy issues. Books, monographs, and shorter studies are commissioned to examine the federal budget, Social Security, regulation, military spending, international trade, and myriad other issues. Major policy conferences are held throughout the year, from which papers are published thrice yearly in the *Cato Journal*. The Institute also publishes the quarterly magazine *Regulation*.

In order to maintain its independence, the Cato Institute accepts no government funding. Contributions are received from foundations, corporations, and individuals, and other revenue is generated from the sale of publications. The Institute is a nonprofit, tax-exempt, educational foundation under Section 501(c)3 of the Internal Revenue Code.

CATO INSTITUTE
1000 Massachusetts Ave., NW
Washington, DC 20001
www.cato.org

CPSIA information can be obtained
at www.ICGtesting.com
Printed in the USA
BVHW030108140919
558360BV00004B/9/P

9 781948 647618